FOUR-TIME NATIO
DIANA LOUISE WEBB

The Butterfly Cometh

Putting the Color Back Into Life

*This is your beautiful life. You only live it once.
Make it hopeful. Make it spectacular.*

Illustrations by Julie Haas

**Outskirts Press, Inc.
Denver, Colorado**

The opinions expressed in this manuscript are solely the opinions of the author and do not represent the opinions or thoughts of the publisher. The author has represented and warranted full ownership and/or legal right to publish all the materials in this book.

The Butterfly Cometh
Putting the Color Back Into Life
All Rights Reserved.
Copyright © 2009 Diana Louise Webb
V3.0

Cover Photo © 2009 by Julie Haas - used with permission.

This book may not be reproduced, transmitted, or stored in whole or in part by any means, including graphic, electronic, or mechanical without the express written consent of the publisher except in the case of brief quotations embodied in critical articles and reviews.

Outskirts Press, Inc.
http://www.outskirtspress.com

ISBN: 978-1-4327-2897-7

Outskirts Press and the "OP" logo are trademarks belonging to Outskirts Press, Inc.

PRINTED IN THE UNITED STATES OF AMERICA

*The country was built on the
belief that each human being
has limitless potential and worth.
Everybody matters.*

George W. Bush
President of the United States of America
April 9, 2008

<u>The Butterfly Cometh</u> offers powerful insight into putting the color back into life. When your azure oasis becomes arid and fades to grey, you may find comfort in realizing you are still basking in the "good life." All you need is a new pair of glasses and a new attitude to delight in the fruition of all the brilliant colors of happiness life invites.

May your life Always Be as Beautiful as Michelangelo Paints!

Diana Louise Webb

ENDORSEMENTS

Here is an eloquently written transformational journey for achieving a world surrounded by love. It's about being happy. Diana's honesty regarding struggles lets us know we are not alone, but that doesn't mean "it's over." Her writing instills that we may always choose to have a great life. This book will change the reader forever as it offers a challenging perspective on living.

CLIFF JOHNSEN, PRESIDENT
EcoAdvantageRE, Inc.

Each one of us is called upon to reach out to others. The personal journey Diana writes about is an incredible odyssey of motivation, reality and transformation. The book outlines a no-holds-barred approach to validating your life. Judging by the quality of many lives today, we, each, might be the wiser to extend a listening ear.

AGUSTIN TORRES, JR., DIRECTOR
Positive Solutions for Life

Diana has a real passion for helping people. The Butterfly Cometh has been a journey nothing short of amazing. It emphasizes Godly understanding amidst what humans call "the game of life." "Bad day" or "good day," sometimes we need to be gently reminded that "this day" is our beautiful life. Nothing else has been promised, whether we're producing records, washing dishes or running a country.

GEORGE HILL, PRESIDENT AND CEO
BNC Entertainment

Yes, we can experience a rewarding life right where we are. Diana does a wonderful job setting forth the intimate relationship between our inner stance, our current circumstances and the resulting quality of being we lead. She makes it apparent that if we don't take a shortcut in the temptation of things that aren't good for us, we will always live in simple abundance. We have the power. What more could we ask?

RACHEL FRANCIS, OWNER/HEAD DESIGNER
CASA ELIZA Interior Designs

This is a book that can be appreciated at several levels. If you are homesick for a more fulfilling life, The Butterfly Cometh discovers a richness which every heart and conscience may experience. Diana unlocks a deep and meaningful chamber of the soul. It's an expedition to be learned from, cherished and shared.

DANIEL WILLIFORD, SYSTEMS ANALYST
DENNIS WILLIFORD, NETWORK ADMINISTRATOR
Advanced Computer and Communications Technologies

I am very impressed with the beauty, holiness and inspiration of the devotions. The hand of God is certainly present and will bring all those who read them closer to the light of Our Lord.

FATHER JOHN NEIMAN, CATHOLIC PRIEST

DEDICATION

I dedicate this book to my mother, Christel Webb. May you always enjoy a first-class seat in the diamond section of the crown of life. I love you, mom.

ACKNOWLEDGMENTS

During a very difficult period in my life, several people made an impression on me which will forever leave an indelible mark of the grace of human kindness. This is not political in nature. It is a humble gratefulness for we will be remembered by how we loved and how well we loved in this world.

To my mom, Christel, and my sister, Rosi, for loving me; Sister Nirmala for your prayers and gentle reminder and living proof that God still performs miracles; Richie for always giving me AMJL4U; Brian for your unconditional love; Col. Gerald Schumacher for having such a beautiful heart; Nicholas and Chris Abnos for your love and support in giving me a great life; Gus Torres for your outstanding contribution to the counseling profession and because you truly care; The Honorable Myron H. Bright, The Honorable Joseph P. Dandurand, The Honorable James P. Gray and The Honorable John T. Curtin, may God bless you abundantly; Father John Neiman for your prayers and great inspiration; Amy Ralston and the CAN-DO foundation for your immense strength and personal integrity; Nora Callahan and the November Coalition for bringing truth to America; Charles Swan for your zeal and assistance; Ruth Carter for always being there with your tow truck and chain; Lori Kavitz for making sure I had more than a pencil to save the world; Deniese Watts for your loads of encouragement; Kathy Kelly for being such an amazing woman; Richard and Tracey Hogg for your beautiful friendship and loving support; Cathy for your concern and help; Cliff for having faith in me; Robert Hall for your prayers;

George Weinbaum for your informative news articles; Juanita Archuleta for being such an awesome friend; Barbara for your love and prayers; Dolores for your loving letters; Terry Lober for your perseverance and understanding; Tom Dawson and John Thompson for the privilege of working for your companies; Tom Stoltz for believing in me; Mary Barr for your compassion and caring sentiments; Dr. Thomas Freeman for your wisdom and sense of humor; Doug Mitchell for your kind thoughts and help; Charity Ryerson for your enthusiasm and commitment; Rachel and Helen Francis for being so fabulous; Tess and Joe for your invaluable friendship; Frank Rinella for your determination and devotion; Nicholas Eyle for offering hope; Michael Smithson for your gifts of the heart; Peter Ninemire for your living example of the ideals by which Ralph Waldo Emerson lived; Donna Reidy for your motivation; Connie Parish for all of your help; David Pryor for your advocacy; Steffen Ufer for your dedication; Sister Pat for being an angel; Rev. Dennis O'Brien for being so gracious; Father Tim, Deacon Ernie and Deacon Chuck for your prayers; David B. Kopel for your support; Michael S. Gelacak for your passion for my cause; Bob Taylor for your assistance; Charles Lauer for being there for me; Brenda Koch for your expert advice; Lexy Cockrell for your help with the graphics; Joe and Teresa McCrudden for your thoughtfulness; Becky Axton for being a terrific friend; the great support of many representatives and senators; and Julie Haas for your brushstrokes which flow as beautifully as Michelangelo paints.

CONTENTS

A Look Within 1
From Big Ben in London, England

Day 1	Dressing Yourself
Day 2	Understanding
Day 3	Wisdom
Day 4	The Violin
Day 5	Boredom
Day 6	Choices
Day 7	Optimism
Day 8	Greed
Day 9	Justice
Day 10	Strength
Day 11	Character
Day 12	Tea Time with Deniese
Day 13	A Great World Mystery
Day 14	Pressure Cooker
Day 15	Mission Possible
Day 16	Self-Destruction
Day 17	Common Sense in a Pantsuit
Day 18	Dodging the Tomahawks
Day 19	Humility
Day 20	Worshipping Aruba
Day 21	Free at Last
Day 22	A Troubled Seat of Conscience

Day 23 .... Starting Over
Day 24 .... Awareness
Day 25 .... The Hope of Life in Death
Day 26 .... Physical Wellness
Day 27 .... Courage
Day 28 .... Two Hearts That Beat as One
Day 29 .... Fortune
Day 30 .... Cherubim
Day 31 .... Control
Day 32 .... Tranquility
Day 33 .... Second Chances
Day 34 .... Even a Brick Wants to be Something
Day 35 .... Purging Your Computer: The Process of Rebirth
Day 36 .... Patriotism
Day 37 .... Temptation
Day 38 .... The Swallowtail Cometh
Day 39 .... Rise up in Grace
Day 40 .... Victory Today is Mine
Day 41 .... For the Love of a Father
Day 42 .... Divine Love
Day 43 .... Humiliation
Day 44 .... Motivation
Day 45 .... Running Against the Wind
Day 46 .... An Evening at the Post
Day 47 .... Patience
Day 48 .... Euphoria
Day 49 .... The Saxophone
Day 50 .... Co-Dependency
Day 51 .... Originality
Day 52 .... The Gift Offering

The Quest for More 63
From the Botanical Gardens of Rio de Janeiro, Brazil

Day 53 .... Snow-in-Summer
Day 54 .... Lemon Bottlebrush
Day 55 .... Hybrid Tea Roses

Day 56 .... Dutchman's-Breeches
Day 57 .... Purple Robe
Day 58 .... Fairy Slipper
Day 59 .... Chamomile
Day 60 .... Coca
Day 61 .... Woolly Yarrow
Day 62 .... Four-Leaf Clover
Day 63 .... Carnation
Day 64 .... Morning Glory
Day 65 .... Claret-Cup Cactus
Day 66 .... Forget-me-Not
Day 67 .... Milkweeds
Day 68 .... English Ivy
Day 69 .... Bleeding Heart
Day 70 .... Creeping Buttercup
Day 71 .... Golden Rod
Day 72 .... Babies'-Breath
Day 73 .... Hollyhock
Day 74 .... Venus's-Flytrap
Day 75 .... Cattail
Day 76 .... Tuberous Begonia
Day 77 .... Dandelion
Day 78 .... Peace Lily
Day 79 .... Indian Paintbrush
Day 80 .... Blue Hyacinth
Day 81 .... Maltese Cross
Day 82 .... Jonquil
Day 83 .... Jacob's-Ladder

Transformation 99
From "Down Under" on Safari in Sydney, Australia

Day 84 .... Bee
Day 85 .... Squirrel
Day 86 .... Barnacle
Day 87 .... Dove
Day 88 .... Beaver

~ xv ~

Day 89	Skunk
Day 90	Iguana
Day 91	Dolphin
Day 92	Bear
Day 93	Lovebirds
Day 94	Monkey
Day 95	Starfish
Day 96	Bulbul
Day 97	Goat
Day 98	Duck
Day 99	Possum
Day 100	Octopus
Day 101	Serpent
Day 102	Pig
Day 103	Sea Crustacean
Day 104	Earwig
Day 105	Kitten
Day 106	Parrot
Day 107	Frog
Day 108	Chicken
Day 109	Doberman Pinscher
Day 110	Deer
Day 111	Bald Eagle
Day 112	Albatross
Day 113	Tiger
Day 114	Firefly
Day 115	Owl
Day 116	Butterfly
Day 117	Mule
Day 118	Lion
Day 119	Ostrich
Day 120	Boll Weevil
Day 121	Crab
Day 122	Beetle
Day 123	Sloth
Day 124	Praying Mantis
Day 125	Wolf
Day 126	Appaloosa

Day 127 .... Euglena
Day 128 .... Siamese Cat
Day 129 .... Blue Heron
Day 130 .... Shrew
Day 131 .... Roadrunner
Day 132 .... Common Blackdevil Deep-Sea Angler
Day 133 .... Laughing Kookaburra
Day 134 .... Sheep
Day 135 .... Pug
Day 136 .... Turtle
Day 137 .... Seahorse
Day 138 .... Chameleon
Day 139 .... Babirusa
Day 140 .... Ant
Day 141 .... Clown Fish
Day 142 .... Chinchilla

Anticipation and Elation 155
From a Hospice Life-Care Center in Āgra, India

Day 143 .... Will the Foundation Break?
Day 144 .... Growing a Beard
Day 145 .... Eyes
Day 146 .... Five-Star Porcelain Veneers on a Bondo Dental Plan
Day 147 .... Acquiring "The Nerve"
Day 148 .... An Empire of Reason
Day 149 .... Internal Secretions
Day 150 .... Achilles' Heel
Day 151 .... Lending a Hand
Day 152 .... Don't Put Your Heart in a Deep Freeze
Day 153 .... Tongue
Day 154 .... Anatomy of a Cell
Day 155 .... If the Nail Breaks, Then...
Day 156 .... Our Defense Mechanisms
Day 157 .... The Signs of Language
Day 158 .... You are the Air I Breathe
Day 159 .... Hair

~ xvii ~

Day 160 .... Chin Up
Day 161 .... Covered in the Precious Blood
Day 162 .... A Trip From the Tibia
Day 163 .... In Hebrew, It's our "Kaph"
Day 164 .... Making Headway
Day 165 .... Behind our Backs
Day 166 .... Walking the Green Mile
Day 167 .... Tasting Life
Day 168 .... It's More Than Skin Deep
Day 169 .... Seeing Beyond the Cornea
Day 170 .... What's Your Connection?
Day 171 .... You Don't Have to be an Athlete to Flex

Introduction

Explore the grand quest of living in the simple excellence for which you are destined!

Too often, we have either chosen not to bring out the Monet within or our paintbrush has dried up and is clogged by our own hurts, unforgiveness and bitter emotions. As you join Christel the butterfly on an impassioned world tour, enjoy the grace of a beautiful life. This trek is designed not only as an inspiration to provide hope and comfort, but also as a passage to a rebirth of self. Delve far beneath what others see and realize the private spirit for what it is. There are times when we are faced with scenarios for which we provide politically correct responses. We do so in order to preserve a wholesome, upstanding image. But do we do the right thing when nobody is looking?

It's easy to put on a facade, but it's peaceful to just be the natural self. To attain such a tranquil existence, we need to like ourselves. When satisfied with self, we are happy and secure in our identity. We, thus, benefit from high self-esteem, establish boundaries and celebrate healthy freedom. We rejoice in liberation from co-dependency, substance abuse and binding chains branded as a troubled mind, envy, regret and worry.

Throughout this sojourn, moisturize the soul. Mend a hurt. Rejuvenate. Travel without so much baggage. Appreciate the "little things." Sleep in serenity. It is the hour to gracefully dance to the extraordinary song of the inner tribunal. Bare your soul to truth, honor and holiness.

We live in a country founded, in part, by a man who was daring enough to say that we were devoted to life, liberty and the pursuit of happiness—he ranked the pursuit of happiness right up there at the top. And beauty and happiness are certainly inextricably tied together.

Claudia "Lady Bird" Johnson
Wife of President Lyndon B. Johnson
February 22, 1965

A LOOK WITHIN
FROM BIG BEN IN LONDON, ENGLAND

As the weather cools, a caterpillar spins a cocoon to shelter itself from the elements before its impressive entrance into the world. Human beings liken in kind as we encase ourselves in walls. The question is what are we keeping in and what are we keeping out? Do we harbor dark secrets and painful memories?

Embark with Christel on the first leg of her travels to the continent of Europe. There you will encounter a tour of vacationers from around the world, all with great stories to tell and dreams to reveal. Search your soul for counsel and direction as you experience a potpourri of life's challenges, fears, desires and undeniable truths.

<u>Day 1</u>:	DRESSING YOURSELF

The eyes are the windows to the soul. Guillaume Du Bartas

Scurrying to dress for a presentation to the world every day, what hidden agenda would air if we could turn ourselves inside out? What exactly is in the core of the inner dressing that appears to others when they look into our eyes?

Imagine the window to your soul . . .

DIANA LOUISE WEBB

What does it look like? Is it an honest opening? Or is it draped in material riches without substance? Is the frame plastic like a credit card—superficial and lacking depth? Or is it constructed of oak—sturdy and reliable? Is your window more of a "what you see is what you get" or is it riddled with layers of false pretenses?

Into what your window opens is just as important as to how it is dressed. A rejoicing heart and a truthful spirit beckons happiness and salvation. An empty, dark heart eaten away with bitterness and driven by dishonesty fogs and solidifies the soul.

Don't woo the invitation to dress the part of a "cover-up." Displaying an artificial mannequin via a deceptive clothing scheme sidesteps God's refining nature. You will, thus, never reap the benefits of your endeavors because you seek to wear a cloak and isolate as opposed to doing out of love.

"Seeming" natural as opposed to "being" natural only "seems" to invoke an opening to increase abundance, but it doesn't. This shallowness cuts the electric cord through which energy flows. Separated from your authentic self, you slip from personal to impersonal love. Dr. Catherine Ponder's book, <u>The Prospering Power of Love</u>, defines those two types of love: "Personal love could be expressed as kindness, tenderness, courtesy, affection, approval, consideration, appreciation, devotion to those in family groups. Impersonal love is basically the ability to get along with people, without personal attachment or emotional involvement." Catherine's rendition on how you can love your way through life, rather than battle your way, is a beautiful example of love's power.

It's time to rehab the window to your soul. First, employ a can of stripper to get rid of any feelings of jealousy, spite, miserliness and defiance. Replenish faith, trust and hope—you have to find meaning for your existence. Replace broken frame parts with solid support. Enjoy simplicity. Remove the inessentials. Dust your window with a soft cloth sprayed with "Love" furniture polish. Rub deeply, but gently, to etch a permanent finish throughout—one comprised of personal love, concentrated momentum and a sincere heart.

THE BUTTERFLY COMETH

Day 2:   UNDERSTANDING

God's gifts put man's best dreams to shame. Elizabeth Barrett Browning

Our bodies are comprised of a miscellany of astonishing substances. The human body contains sufficient lime to whitewash a small shed, the equivalent in carbon of a 28-pound bag of coke, phosphorus tantamount to make 2,200 match heads, one spoonful of sulfur, ample iron to construct a one-inch nail and approximately one ounce of other metals.[1] Although hidden, the substances serve a purpose whether we recognize it or not.

God, as the architect of our lives, designed us. Not only did God design us in the physical sense, but He also gave rise to the faith within us. To erect and assemble our lives without Him is for naught. God is the Builder and when we exclude Him, our efforts toil in vain.

Just as carbon, phosphorus, sulfur and iron have a purpose, so too, does God have for each and every living creature. We may never understand why our bodies have the capacity to engineer 2,200 match heads inasmuch as we may never understand God's purpose for us until we reach the other side.

When you invest in God, your citizenship vests in Heaven. He who has the power to bring everything under His control will transform your lowly body so that you will be like His glorious body. It will be at that very instant life will fan out full circle and you will come to know pure understanding.

The plans of the Lord stand firm forever, the purposes of His heart through all generations. Psalm 33:11

Day 3:   WISDOM

Suffering will never be completely absent from our lives. If we accept it with faith, we are given the opportunity to share the passion of Jesus and show Him our love. Mother Teresa

---

[1] Reader's Digest Book of Facts. New York: Reader's Digest Association, Inc., 1985.

Diana Louise Webb

Growing up in Germany in the 1940's my mother witnessed the horrors of the Nazi regime. My grandfather once made a negative comment about Hitler in jest and was almost taken away by the Gestapo to a concentration camp.

When Germany lost the war, it disintegrated. There was no food in the stores; the shelves were bare. At age ten, my mother and her two siblings learned that a military installation was located nearby. American soldiers occupied the quarters and it was evident that they had food and supplies. My mother, along with other German children, took containers from home and put them through the fence where the armed forces ate their meals. A trashcan was nearby outside. The children reached out for the soldiers to dump their leftovers into the containers instead of into the garbage can, which many of them gladly obliged. Some even loaded their plates with extra helpings so that they could give away more food.

However, a select few poked fun at the German children for reaching out for their discards. Sometimes, they took pictures of this desperate sight. My mother still remembers the embarrassment.

Later on, there were heavenly times for the children. The soldiers spoiled them with chocolates, fruit, chewing gum, candy, cookies and other goodies--and balloons and rides in their jeeps. My mother envisioned America as a wonderful country.

Many years later, my mother met my father, an American stationed in Germany. They married and moved to the United States.

As I reflect upon the actions of some of the soldiers snickering at the misfortune of the German children, I realize that one cannot hold an entire class of people responsible for the acts of a few individuals. Generalizations created about a segment of the population, a country, a class of people or particular organizations based on the conduct of only a few members are not fair assessments.

My mother told me that America is even a more wonderful country than she had pictured as a child. The irony is that many of the freedoms we enjoy every day are taken for granted. We are able to move about freely; bathe in hot water; and take part in a constitution that allows for and promotes life, liberty and the pursuit of happiness. The democratic process gives us each a voice.

Our Founding Fathers established a firm foundation from which to build a great nation. The beauty is that we are afforded the right to disagree and we have the ability to 'choose.' We are a country that exhibits God's greatest love—a people who lay down their lives for one another daily. We have seen this chivalry in the heroic deeds our citizens perform such as fighting fires and making our streets safe from crime.

We have witnessed the true red, white and blue in liberating another country from oppression. These selfless acts are what makes America stand out as a nation that welcomes the promises it made. As Americans, we do so with hearts filled with love, compassion and honor. We do so not only on American soil, but also in other countries, as we recognize that not just Americans alone are privileged and deserving. Dominion and torment rule not. Justice, freedom and happiness are for the world.

In the fabric of life, we are either nicely embroidering the linen for others or we are fraying the Harris Tweed. Which one are you choosing?

Day 4:   THE VIOLIN

The canary is like our soul. It sees bars around it, but instead of despairing, it sings, and see, one day its song shall break the bars. Nikos Kazantzakis, Saint Francis

The Stradivarius—outstanding craftsmanship, superb varnish and a beautiful shape and proportion. Antonio Stradivari, its creator, lived during the seventeenth/eighteenth century, and remained unsurpassed in quality as an Italian violinmaker. During his career, he masterpieced about 1,000 string instruments. Of these, 635 violins are still in existence.

When we marvel at something so beautiful on the outside, we cannot help but wonder how the intricate workings sound. For anyone who has heard a Stradivarius played, this is easily answered. The showpiece renders an incomparable blend of strength and sweetness of composition—an opening into what Heaven might be like.

The true essence of the violin is captured in the passions of Hafiz (1320-1389): "When the violin can forgive the past, it starts singing. When the violin can forgive every wound caused by others, the heart starts singing." This forgiving grace is captured spiritually through the wisdom of Sundar Singh. Singh recapped that the fitness of our hearts and thoughts to receive God's spirit is like that of violin strings. If they are properly tuned, in harmony with one another, then the touch of the bow produces magnificent music. If not, there is only discord.

Whenever your heart is ready to receive God's spirit, like the Stradivarius, Heavenly solidarity and joyous harmony will impart—both in this life and the next.

Day 5:   BOREDOM

When there are no fish in one spot, cast your net in another. Chinese Proverb

If a deck of cards could speak, what would they say? Would they simply cough from billows of smoke at the casino? Would they compare uncomfortable positions from lying around gathering dust in a household cabinet? Would they boast when everything fell in place and the "big one" came to pass?

We operate much like a deck of cards. When things are rolling favorably, we relish the fanfare. But when a less desired existence fills every side of life, we fold. We lie down and lose contact with the universe. When disgruntled, we tend to complain and grow wearisome and uninterested in the current agenda. Whether it be a failing relationship, an unstimulating job or a dissatisfying view of self, we focus on the negative points instead of delighting in the good. We embrace a flatness which causes us to quarantine ourselves in our own little world. Our minds, mothballed in humdrum indifference, lead us to crave excitement and rouse anything to block out our contemporary being. Loathed to face our boring reality, we find substitutes for the monotony. We seek redress for the bad card hand we believe we were dealt.

But truth tells us it is not what life dishes out which denotes quality. It is the magic we develop with the aces God gave us.

The next time boredom yawns your direction, pick up a deck of cards. Divvy the cards on the table and search for the aces: the ace of diamonds, the ace of hearts, the ace of spades and the ace of clubs.

THE BUTTERFLY COMETH

Lay them across in a row. Remember, it is in your power to make each day a diamond no matter how dim the circumstances. You have the choice to offer your heart and hands in service and not in sin. If you don't own one, buy a spade to dig through the prophecy of doom which buries you. Finally, join a club—one that features a hobby you like.

"Suit" up on spirit! Life can never be dull when you hold a handful of aces.

Day 6:   CHOICES

Look at life through the windshield, not the rearview mirror. Proverb

At the grocery store, Alley, the director of the health spa at which I exercise, bumped my cart in the produce aisle. Out of sorts, Alley asked to reveal a disturbing dream she had the previous evening. It bothered her so much she needed to share it with someone. After hearing what was more like a nightmare, I, too, suffered icy chills.

Alley found herself on a pontoon boat taking a pleasure cruise. Although married, she went sailing unaccompanied on this particular outing. Nine other passengers joined. Without warning, turbulence overshadowed the vessel and it sprung a leak. The first mate summoned the Coast Guard. It dispatched immediately, but the weight of those onboard proved too heavy to outlast the time it would take for help to arrive. Hence, all luggage and supplies were thrown overboard. Still, at least two people needed to be removed off the pontoon. If not, all passengers would die.

An elderly couple stepped forward and offered up their lives as they had already lived abundantly. In a heart-wrenching decision, the passengers agreed this was the best option. But somebody had to lower the couple into the raw, biting lake. Alley was the only one strong enough to do it. As Alley agonized over the dilemma, she abruptly woke up.

Who has the right to decide who lives and who dies? Is one life more important than another? Does man have the right to assist in suicide?

The naked reality is "we" do not run the show. Human life cannot be part of our "throw away" culture. We are not to play God under any circumstances and we were not designed to do so. It takes someone bigger than we are to command and rule. When we are too busy doing God's work, God can't work.

Melinda Ribner urges us to remember, "God is sustaining our life and everything else in creation. We are born into this world and we will die and leave this world. Our first breath and our last breath, the two most important events in life, are not in our conscious control. Because our breathing is automatic and involuntary, it is easy to forget about the gift of breath—gift of God." It is God's gift to give, not ours.

Reality dictates that we live events every day which back us up against a rocky boulder. But with time and stick-to-itiveness, we can shinny out of the crevice. With each minute that passes so, too, does each affliction pass. The passageway is the door to the "Greater Life." And as we scale, we must not forget to look under foot--God is closer than we think.

Still in the business of performing miracles, let God take the controlling interest of your life. Give Him the power. But not only the power, give Him the glory and the honor. When you play God, you play with fire. The rain will never come and you will perish in the flames.

Day 7:   OPTIMISM

I'm so optimistic I'd go after Moby Dick in a rowboat and take the tartar sauce with me. Tony Campolo

It's 6:00 a.m. The buzzing alarm doesn't miss a beat. It was a late night and the last thing you want to do is come out from under the covers and trout off to your nine-to-fiver. One toe peeks from beneath the comforter. Ooh wee, is it ever cold! You quickly yank it back in and hit the "snooze" button. You long to be just where you are for the rest of the morning.

Reclining back for a brief doze, you find yourself on a surfboard. This is no ordinary surfboard; it is a fabulous flying machine. Propelled only by your buoyancy, this flashy work of art is zooming through the solar system. Your self-assurance magnanimously fuels the vessel. Smoke sambas off the tail fin in a unique motif.

THE BUTTERFLY COMETH

Capable and competent, perfectly poised on the board, you navigate between Mercury and Venus. You are sizzling with terrific expectations. Smokin' with heart and oomph, your colorful strobe imbues the stratosphere. It is evident your travels are always sunny as you sport your new galactic visor.

Momentously, you are hurled back into your cozy bed. You open your eyes and give the blankets a swift punt. Bouncing out of your pajamas, you put a little hip in your dip and toss up the window sash. In a zany German accent, you belt out a celebrated, "Guten Morgen Ihr alle!"[2]

You then dress for success.

Whether we are cognizant of it or not, each day is a very good day. Majorie Holmes spurs our memory to connect with a pure spirit of "a very good day." She writes, " ... For it's been filled with life. The life you have given me to cope with, and to contribute to. And I wouldn't want to have missed it, not a single moment of it. Thank you, God, for this good day."

This is a day which you have to experience for yourself. A disciple once complained, "You tell us stories, but you never divulge their meaning to us." The master answered, "How would you like it if someone offered you fruit and chewed it up before you received it?"

Looking on to today, are you living the plans God envisioned for you? Are you seeking Him with all you have? Open your hands before God and He will work everything out for the Lord is always faithful to His word.

As you step out onto your big adventure gondola, let life amuse you. You earned it. Remember, there will always be something firm to plant your feet on.

Day 8:   GREED

The love of money was what motivated Judas to sell Jesus. Mother Teresa

---

[2] German for "Good morning you all!"

Diana Louise Webb

In 1977, <u>Mother Jones</u> promulgated an article relating to the inherent dangers of the fuel tank designs in particular models of certain automobiles. A journalist cited internal manufacturer documents proving knowledge that the designs would result in gas tank explosions during rear-end collisions. The company released the cars into the market anyway. A cost/benefit analysis study advanced the theory that the manufacturer found it would be cheaper to pay off lawsuits of unsuspecting burn and death victims rather than to recall the cars.

Subsequent to the report, an Orange County jury awarded a victim $125,000,000 in punitive damages against the car company.[3] The injured man suffered terrible burns in a rear-end collision while he was a passenger in one of the defective vehicles. The car erupted into flames at an impact of 28 mph. The jury rationalized the verdict by agreeing that it was only fair for the punitive damages to be more than the automobile corporation made in profit since inception of that particular car: $124,000,000.

To consider a beloved life as "collateral damage" to be rectified by the almighty dollar is just one example of how the "love of money" corrupts people and society. But we all have done it at one time or another: broken the rules of life. Simply put, we don't follow the arrow between sensible living and how we actively live. Early on, we defy the norms of behavior. Next, we put fairness at the bottom of the deepest ocean. We exalt a lie to the highest mountain. Then, we sit back and wonder why it is so difficult to "find" God.

Isn't life funny inasmuch as we keep reveling, "He is coming! He is coming!" when, in fact, He is here.

Understanding genuine happiness is to keep company with the timeless joy which comes without cost. This type of joy is gleaned in the beauty of a single blade of grass—rich in its potential for growth and renewal; in the gentle cadence of the wings of a swan—producing beatific acoustics giving one's soul a new dimension in the world of sound; the ebb and flow of an ocean—instilling complexity and depth to the introspective process of exploring the inner self.

---

[3] The award was reduced to $3.5 million by the trial judge.

THE BUTTERFLY COMETH

"Someday," said Teilhard de Chardin, "After mastering the winds, the waves, the tides, and gravity, we shall harness for God the energies of love and then, for the second time in the history of the world, man will have discovered fire."

Are you one of the chosen?

Day 9:   JUSTICE

Actions will be judged according to their results. Mohammad

The south of Scotland is an opulent place to visit. The historical aspects are spectacular, especially the ruins of the Scottish abbey at Melrose. Edinburgh, Scotland, offers a splendid view as well as scrumptious eateries. The relics of centuries gone remain preserved for the enjoyment of both the natives and the visitors.

The Grassmarket was one of the busiest markets in Medieval Edinburgh. A castle loomed high over the market place. To the far east stood a building approximately six stories in height. Because the Gothic city was densely packed, about 10,000 people living on less than one square mile, the homes were built on the side of a mountain. By Medieval standards, they tended to be very tall, some rising as many as fourteen stories.

Of interest, the rich, the middle class and the poor often lived in the same building. But in the Middle Ages, there were no elevators. Since the affluent did not revel climbing fourteen flights of stairs, it was the poor who lived at the top. Imagine the difficulty alone of hauling water to the upper floors in the days before plumbing. Shops occupied the ground floor and the rich lived just above the shops.

Nowadays, it is the wealthy who reside in penthouses on the top floor. Society holds those who are "well off" in much higher esteem than serfs or servants who work in the basement.

In God's eyes, it doesn't matter whether we live upstairs or downstairs. God is not a respecter of persons. He will judge everyone the same—by what is in their hearts.

Don't waste your gifts of the heart. Discover Jesus in the blind, the crippled, the poor and the lame. Those who live by the spirit of love will know joy and harmony in the everlasting Dance of the Cosmos.

DIANA LOUISE WEBB

Glory awaits you within the citadel, within the City of Lights. Psalm 87

Day 10:   STRENGTH

You are the salt of the earth. Matthew 5:13

The year: 1641. Samuel Winslow from Massachusetts made history by being the first colonist to be issued a patent. Awarded for a process he developed to manufacture salt, Winslow recognized the value in a mineral many people commonly overlook.

Salt is a very important commodity to man, but if salt loses its strength, it is no longer usable for anything. As humans, our "salt" is our strength. Without physical strength, we cannot engage in labor or activities. Without mental strength, we are unable to outlast bad luck and taxing days. Without strength of spirit, we orphan the heart that we depend on for survival and emotional sustenance.

Spiritual advisor, Randy Phillips, shepherds us in faith by reaffirming that "God brings His vision to fulfillment not through our strength, but by His strength working in us." An amazing phenomenon is just how much strength we truly possess. We are a lot stronger than we think we are.

When forced to face the unthinkable, we verbalize that we would rather simply die on the spot. But did we? No, we didn't die. There we were—alive and kicking, not just that day, but the next and the next and the next. Yes, we were AOA [Alive on Arrival].

A dear woman, Ruth, whom I am proud to call my friend, is a courageous and forgiving person. And she has certainly had her share of testing of strength. Ruth lost her beautiful daughter, Casey, at the young age of twenty-one. Asleep in the backseat of a car, Casey was ejected during a drunk driving accident and died on impact. This tragedy occurred thirty-seven days after Ruth's son-in-law committed suicide.

Mourning the loss of a child is a shock that can only be comprehended by a parent. Even then, it is never fully understood. Working through the hurt is lengthy and sorrowful. Unfortunately, there are no courses on how to make a life—just how to make a living.

THE BUTTERFLY COMETH

There were many days that Ruth wanted to surrender. "God, you can no longer hold my life in your hands. Your tests are too much for me." In that decisive moment, God said, "My precious child, I will never leave you." With God watching over her, Ruth didn't succumb. She never lost her salt. With God's help, Ruth nourished and strengthened her salt. She remained AOA.

Eventually, the intoxicated driver responsible for Casey's death was brought to justice. In merciful dispensation, Ruth wrote to the sentencing judge requesting leniency for the offender. In a letter written with clarity and compassion, she opened her heart to the notion that individuals with substance abuse problems need help, not punishment. Rehabilitation should replace retribution.

The world lost a dear child when Casey died, but through her mother, Ruth, her memory will live on forever.

This story can be one which emphasizes the precious nature of life, the importance of salt, and why love and time matter.

Yes, you have been given a life to handle and have a say in. Be the salt of the earth. The natural reverence that emanates from an awareness of the sacred in and around you is obedience to the breath of life. Alive with spirit, recognize God's call to "curve" to His will. Be expectant. Stay determined. Have no regrets. Lutz into every episode of life AOA.

In loving memory of Casey
04/17/79 - 02/19/01
Casey, I will always remember you. Love, mom

Day 11:   CHARACTER

Reconsider your definitions. We are prone to judge success by the index of our salaries or the size of our automobiles rather than by the quality of our service and relationship to mankind. Martin Luther King, Jr.

It is your weekend to work at the local food pantry for the underprivileged. Named on a rotating schedule with three other volunteers, your shift is three hours every third Saturday distributing free groceries.

On this particular Saturday, you have front row seats to your favorite recording artist's final music tour. This is a once-in-a-lifetime chance. You have never seen your star live in concert. As an added bonus, backstage passes have been included with the tickets.

No one is available to switch hours at the food pantry. If you don't show up, the pantry stays closed and the needy meet a shut door until the next weekend. However, none of the other volunteers will ever find out you didn't work.

Do you go to the concert?

Enticed by an attractive alternative to a set plan, whether we stand on our word or conviction centers around "character." Our personal constitution guides us and shapes us. When we want to "look good" for others, we usually do what is right. But do we do the honorable thing when we are not under public scrutiny?

Thomas Macaulay styled 'character' as "what a man would do if he knew he would never be found out." How much consideration do you afford in that regard? In the light of day, it is not difficult to appear decent and noble. That said, we cannot conceal our insincerity or keep up a guise forever.

'Two' are privy to our actual intentions—we are one; God, the other. When we align ourselves with a bona fide objective in Christ and put all false fronts aside, we are able to procure equilibrium. Anchored in morality, we are not wrapped up in lies and deceit.

If you are destined to inherit the throne, walk in faith-filled integrity. Your actions take on the persona of your conscience which is formed by your faith. When faithful until death, as you stand at The Last Judgment, the Great Sculptor's hand molds you into the likeness of Christ. Sharing in His kingdom, you will not just be in Heaven, you will be part of Heaven—a union with Christ Himself.

Day 12:   TEA TIME WITH DENIESE

I want to be the sun because I want to shine and bring light into people's lives. Deniese Watts

What would it be like to be . . .

THE BUTTERFLY COMETH

- a Venetian blind. What would you let in and what would you keep out?

- the wind ... to travel all over. If it got too cold, you could float to the wonderful sands of Portugal.

- a radio ... to broadcast sweet music and the news to keep everyone informed.

- an emery board ... to sooth out the rough edges and shape tips.

- a yardstick ... to show the people how to measure up.

- a filter ... to deterge all contamination.

- Da Vinci's <u>Mona Lisa</u>. As the song says, "Ain't nothing like the real thing."

- a coffee cup ... to get a taste of cappuccino and a kiss every morning.

- Father Time ... where there is neither a beginning nor an end.

- "The Rock" ... in front of His tomb ...

<u>Day 13</u>:   A GREAT WORLD MYSTERY

How far have we come in man's long pilgrimage from darkness toward light? Dwight D. Eisenhower

The age of the Sphinx is one of the world's most baffling riddles. Located in Egypt, the Sphinx possesses deluding attributes. Peculiarly intriguing is how the ancient people built the Sphinx and when. The face itself is a transfixing feature—possibly modeled after the pharaoh, Chephren, who ruled from 2556 to 2530 B.C.

Archaeologists determined that many of the distinguishing hallmarks of the Sphinx have been worn away—so severely that the damage could not have been the result of windblown sand. Would this mean that at one time the Sphinx was buried at the bottom of the sea?

The Sphinx remains an architectural rarity lending credence that our distant ancestors held far more technical knowledge than for which we give them credit.

That principle may be applied by way of comparison to the elder members of our society. How often do we push them to the side and not recognize the rarity of their value? In <u>A Message For Humanity</u>, K. Martin-Kuri posits that as one approaches the years beyond seventy, the veils of Heaven are particularly open to the soul. This signifies that these priceless gems have the opportunity to be of unprecedented service to humankind. They can contribute their most vital work: to offer wisdom and experience to the young.

<u>Friends of Silence</u> reiterates K. Martin-Kuri's practicalities and poses two questions which merit pensive meditation: 1) How can we prepare for the most critical years by maintaining we are going to shut down our engines? 2) What have we done by limiting those persons who have the most to offer to our society?

This eve, think.

<u>Day 14</u>:   PRESSURE COOKER

Nobody, as long as he moves among the chaotic currents of life, is without trouble. Carl Jung

We have each lived those exasperating moments when we resist saying the wrong thing at the right time. We appease our hearts and practice the paragon: a closed mouth inserts no foot.

Nevertheless, the internal aftermath hurls a plethora of emotions into a tailspin.

In refusing to give way to discourteous words and affronting digs, the pressure mounts. An outward manifestation of ruthless dissatisfaction surges. We are ready to blow!

And when we can't or don't, our subdued rotten feelings hammer out a concave depression in which to store hate and sarcasm. We trudge through this medley of sludge, slaves encased in a poppling teakettle. Before we know it, we are spent.

THE BUTTERFLY COMETH

But when we are spiritually enriched, God makes known His divinity and the fullness of His being so that we have all our pleasures in Him. The hedonistic self-consummation slowly departs. We experience a calmness and sense of contentment.

The next time you have the urge to sleep with a corpse, keep the deadened feelings where they belong—in a cemetery for those who can't rise above it all.

Day 15:   MISSION POSSIBLE

One small step for man, one giant step for mankind. Neil A. Armstrong

On July 20, 1969, the entire world watched as Neil A. Armstrong, Michael Collins and Edwin 'Buzz' Aldrin, Jr., traveling aboard the Apollo 11 lunar module Eagle, became the first men to set foot on the moon. What a feeling of exhilaration it must have been to be part of such an important mission.

We, too, have missions in our lives for which we should feel connected and important to be part of a team. Energy flows in abundance when we join with others to accomplish worthy goals.

On Monday, June 21, 2004, another outstanding achievement for science transpired when SpaceShipOne completed the first privately financed manned space flight. Pilot, Michael W. Melvill's spacecraft climbed to the end of the earth's atmosphere which denotes the beginning of space. The altitude—62.2 miles: the eternal horizon where space is dark, there is no sound and objects float.

When we go forth in the quest of a mission, we commence with an idea. The idea procreates into a leap of faith from darkness—concepts in the making, churning without a purpose and without a voice, just like SpaceShipOne's voyage. But then direction materializes. The theory, the plan, the design take form and shape.

In the space industry, a voice was created to enable further exploration and continued travel. This voice will some day lead to a future where tourists will be able to hover high above the earth, take in all the sights and levitate in a no-gravity zone. The milestone began as a small inspiration almost forty years ago. None of this could have been possible without the teamwork of the participants.

Diana Louise Webb

As you journey in pursuit of your mission, experience the adventure with the same rocket fuel as Neil, Buzz, Michael and Mike did. Welcome the thoughts and opinions of your teammates. Keep an open mind. Appreciate the ideas submitted by others. Aim high!

Keep in the forefront of your mind that although the passage may be peppered with patches of darkness, the light of Christ will always burn brightly. He will guide you if you acknowledge Him in all you do.

Day 16:   SELF-DESTRUCTION

My brush stroke has no system at all. I hit the canvas with irregular strokes which I leave as they are. Patches of thick color, spots of canvas left uncovered, maddening I'm sure to people with fixed ideas about technique. Vincent van Gogh, 1853-1890

Misunderstood, ingenious and unappreciated until too late, Vincent van Gogh proved to be one of the world's finest artists. Born in 1853, Van Gogh grew up in Holland. He was regarded as a "different" child, not gifted.

At sixteen, Vincent opted for work as an apprentice art dealer, a vocation which did not last long. He then followed a calling to evangelism and lived amongst an impoverished community. Finding himself penniless, at twenty-seven, Van Gogh broached a career as an artist at the encouragement of his brother, Theo. He spent fifteen months in Arles in the South of France which represented the climax of his profession. In 444 days, he painted 200 paintings and 100 drawings, including <u>Sunflowers</u>, a masterpiece that sold for $40,000,000 at an auction in March of 1987.[4]

In spite of it all, Vincent never achieved happiness, nor did he ever discover a comfortable spot of being. He longed to devise a colony of artists—"a collective studio of painters to be our united strength against poverty and bad health," but he gave up. Instead, he simply traveled around unattached from society, gradually asphyxiating his spirit.

---

[4] Only one Van Gogh painting sold during his lifetime, the price was the equivalent of $80.00.

THE BUTTERFLY COMETH

Van Gogh's continued melancholy state manifested itself in the physical realm when at age thirty-seven, he shot himself in a cornfield. Dying two days later, Vincent fulfilled his premonition of life being a "short" blink of time.[5]

French Impressionist, Claude Monet, figuratively drew Van Gogh's life as a sorrowful languishing away of talent. He voiced, "How could a man who so loved flowers and light, and has rendered them so well ... have managed to be so unhappy?"

Perhaps it is the gaps of doubt which make faith for something better to come in the afterlife possible. For without doubt, why would we need faith? But doubts must be acknowledged, accepted, embraced and pushed past before our faith is strong enough, not just to talk about, but also to sustain. Faith is not making religious-sounding noises in the daytime. It's asking innermost self-questions at night—and then getting up the next morning and going to work.

During your journey, keep the important element—happiness—close. As long as you keep the faith, don't quit and continue moving, no matter how slowly you go, no matter how many times you fall, you will eventually tap into your promise. Only then will you savor the sweetness of the corn on the cob. What a pity some stare so long at the husk that they never notice the breathtaking ambrosial tiara sprouting through the stalk.

Day 17:   COMMON SENSE IN A PANTSUIT

Don't ask, "What if it doesn't work?" Instead, ask, "How will I feel if I don't even try?" Suzanne Zoglio

We are the first to give advice, but the last to take it. We are the first to complain that our steak is too tough, but what about when we need a little tenderizing ourselves? We can figure out the value of pi in geometry, but we can't figure out the value of a dollar. We can appreciate the artistic talent of Rembrandt, but we can't appreciate what we have until it's gone. We will throw out the kitchen trash

---

[5] Searchinger, Gene (Producer/Director). <u>In a Brilliant Light: Van Gogh in Arles</u>. [film] New York, NY: The Office of Film and Television of the Metropolitan Museum of Art, 1984.

without any problem, but we won't relinquish the garbage built up in our minds and hearts.

Common sense lays bare that the progression of learning/doing/teaching happens in synchronicity, but it has to be a give-and-take operation. Harry Emerson Fosdick best illustrated such coordination, and the lack thereof, in <u>The Meaning of Service</u> which he wrote in 1920. "The Sea of Galilee and the Dead Sea are made of the same water. It flows down, clear and cool, from the heights of Hermon and the roots of the cedars of Lebanon. The Sea of Galilee makes beauty of it, for the Sea of Galilee has an outlet. It gets to give. It gathers in its riches that it may pour them out again to fertilize the Jordan plain. But the Dead Sea with the same water makes horror. For the Dead Sea has no outlet. It gets to keep."

Everything we need to know is not found in a book. We need to take action. Subsisting solely through the pages of a "how-to" manual only grants us the satisfaction of nibbling the crumbs that fall from the dinner table. We never taste the banquet. We are graced with special presents from our Heavenly Father which are to be shared; whether it be book knowledge, street smarts, skills or just "being there." Sometimes we can change things and sometimes we must just accept what is there—and still shine throughout the sojourn. But we have to offer something and jump in with hands-on preparation.

As believers in our Lord, we are guaranteed perfect conformity to Jesus at His next coming. However, God hopes that we do not passively wait until we enter the gates of Heaven to undergo such a miraculous transformation. He wants us to grow in Christ in 'this world.'

Rise up off your proverbial throne and quit being a stranger to a rewarding life. When you live by the side of happiness instead of in the midst of it, life passes you by. Then when your 'service' appears, you will not be ready.

Today: Shine!

<u>Day 18</u>: DODGING THE TOMAHAWKS

Let Hercules himself do what he may, the cat will mew, and the dog will have his day. <u>Hamlet</u>

THE BUTTERFLY COMETH

The Tomahawk Club operates at all levels of the socioeconomic status. It is the universal alliance that binds us all in one way or another. There are Junior, Senior and Charter members. At the crest, the Platinum Circle vests.

We, each, have thrown a tomahawk or received one in the back at some point in our lives.

God blew life into Adam; thus, distinguishing us as living beings as opposed to inert objects. As we inhale and exhale, we connect with God and one another. We take in the sea of air which swirls through the lungs of both our friends and our enemies. When we breathe, we become one in life; one in spirit.

We cannot afford to be drawn off center to the detriment of our fellow man. To set in motion a chain of digressive thoughts and motions will eventually destroy us. In our favor, the more completely a man dies to self, the more he begins to live for God. Fourteenth-century German abbot, St. Thomas á Kempis, who fathered <u>The Imitation of Christ</u>, pointed out that God desires for us to learn to bear trials without comfort so that we will yield wholly to Him and grow more humble through tribulation. We must live a dying life. When the self's spurious temperament is diminished and we feel weak, it is then that we are unquestionably strong. We possess a self-emptied soul in which Christ's power may descend and fill us. We, thereby, stand in 'God's knowing' and in 'God's love.'

When you decide to throw a tomahawk or duck to avoid one, beseech the All-Powerful to excavate the layers of self. Ask that He permanently sedate the whirlwind of hate, envy, vengeance and hurtful thoughts which precipitated picking up the tomahawk in the first place. Recognize the "I AM" as the greatest good and beckon Him to lead you to stillness.

Offer your body as a living sacrifice, holy and pleasing to God—this is your spiritual act of worship. Do not conform any longer to the pattern of this world, but be transformed by the renewing of your mind. Then you will be able to test and approve what God's will is—His good, pleasing and perfect will (Romans 12:1-2).

As you ask Jesus to create in you a pure heart, you are exactly the one whom He is looking for to make a fresh start. Do not ignore God because you feel sinful or unworthy. When you are down to nothing, God is up to something. The Lord is waiting to be gracious to you.

Diana Louise Webb

<u>Day 19</u>:   HUMILITY

Blessed are those who are poor in spirit; they will inherit the earth.
Matthew 5:3

I am one of Mother Teresa's greatest admirers. Her humility, selflessness and service to the poorest of the poor in India provide a constant reminder that there should be no vainglory in work.

Mother Teresa cheerfully accepted all God sent. When she died, I was filled with downheartedness, but I know God did not want that. Sister Nirmala was chosen to continue God's work in resuming Mother Teresa's humanitarian efforts in India and throughout the world. She preferred "Sister" as opposed to "Mother" as she felt there was only one Mother—Mother Teresa. A holy and living paradigm of love, Sister Nirmala is an extraordinary woman.

In August, 2002, I received news that my mammogram during a physical exam demonstrated an abnormality. An ultrasound was ordered for further evaluation. I was devastated to learn that a possible malignant tumor was being obscured by dense tissue, necessitating immediate surgery.

I wrote to Sister Nirmala appealing for prayer. She responded to my concerns with not only an outpouring of prayer, but also an invitation to join the sisters in their "humble works for His little ones," in Calcutta, India. Elaborating further on the mission, Sister Nirmala wrote, "... Our Shishu Bhavan just down the street from the Mother House is full of children awaiting adoption or recovering from malnutrition or other illness. Loving hearts and hands are always needed there. And we also have a home for children with disabilities. Nothing special is needed—just contact us when you are ready to come. God's ways are always so full of love even in our sorrow and sufferings. He is able to draw out much good. God is working in your soul and He will do great things in and through you. Pray, be at peace and wait on the Lord."

When I received the heartwarming reply, a sense of serenity enveloped my being.

Another ultrasound was administered and revealed "no visible well-defined cyst or solid mass." The radiologist advised me that there was a "lack of correlation between the prior mammographic findings and the current ultrasound examination" which could not be explained through medical science. The former depicted a mass not substantiated by the latter. Intercessory prayer brought about my miraculous healing.

When we approach impasses with sincere prayer in a humble, holy way, God moves the Canadian Rockies. By practicing humility, we free ourselves from boastfulness and narcissism which destroy the soul. By exercising humbleness, we don't depreciate ourselves. We still possess self-dignity and proper respect, and espouse Christian pride.

When our ego becomes too commanding, our conscience becomes hard-boiled. We clinch self-centered behavior and evince insensitivity toward others.

In her Psalms for Praying, Nan Merrill captures the essence of humbleness in Psalm 18, "Those who love truth will see your Light; those who walk in justice, will see your Mercy; those who live with integrity, will see You in all they meet; but those whose path is crooked, who walk on the low road, will live in the shadows of fear. The humble are always close to You, the haughty, too distracted to see, will one day fall."

Imagine Jesus sitting beside you. With each transaction, concerted effort or spoken word, WWJD (what would Jesus do)? What would He say? How would He act?

Now, it's your turn. Do it.

Day 20:   WORSHIPPING ARUBA

Every human being has, like Socrates, an attendant spirit; and wise are they who obey its signals. If it does not always tell us what to do, it always cautions us what not to do. Lydia M. Child

Nineteen miles off the coast of Venezuela lies the beautiful island of Aruba. While referred to as a tropical paradise, Aruba is actually a desert. Nonetheless, the beaches boast gorgeous white sand lending themselves out all year around to "sun worshippers" on vacation.

The term "sun worshipper" is somewhat a misnomer, as sunbathers do not actually "worship" the sun; they simply bask in its opulence for endless hours, a satisfying and pleasurable pastime.

DIANA LOUISE WEBB

When it comes to true "worship," there is only one whom we should venerate—our Father in Heaven. God's law forbids practicing idolatry toward other supposed powers. God does not share His glory. The use of idols, real or imaginary, runs afoul to the Ten Commandments which prohibit bowing to or serving graven images.

Originally etched on two stone tablets, the Ten Commandments were received by Moses on Mount Sinai as the ten basic laws of the Law covenant.

As you carry on living life, keep all of God's laws sacred. Realize that the most important commandment is to love the Lord with your whole heart. Then love your neighbor as yourself. If you will do just that, He will insure a walkway for good things to follow—one leading to a never-ending paradise with more stunning brilliance than offered by the sunniest beaches of Aruba.

Day 21:   FREE AT LAST

Let the Force be with you. Obi Wan Kenobi

Every year in the United States, 2.3 million women are severely assaulted by their spouses; 1,300 killed.[6] Domestic violence knows no boundaries. It violates human dignity and fails to honor respect.

Violence is a learned behavior. We imitate what we see and to what we are exposed. Parents who were abused by their parents are six times more likely to abuse their own children.[7] Alcohol and drug usage, inability to cope with stress and lack of education contribute to domestic assaults.

If you are a victim of abuse, the first riser to free yourself is to admit that you are being violated and that you deserve to be treated with dignity. You have the right to feel safe from physical harm, especially in your own home.[8]

---

[6] Brinegar, Jerry. Breaking Free from Domestic Violence. Minnesota: CompCare Publishers, 1992.
[7] Whitaker, Carl. From Psyche to System: The Evolving Therapy of Carl Whitaker. New York, NY: Guilford Press, 1982.
[8] Brinegar, supra, n. 5.

THE BUTTERFLY COMETH

Being a victim of domestic violence doesn't necessarily mean the relationship is over, whether it be spouse/spouse, parent/child or boyfriend/girlfriend. Through prayer, intense therapy, support groups and a reformation of a hardened heart, the relationship may be salvageable. This is only possible if you assure yourself that there will be zero tolerance for battering in the reconciliation.

Help is out there. Women's shelters provide protection for both victims and their children. Hotlines are available in all phonebooks, the Internet and through directory assistance. Many women stay in abusive situations because they feel their options are so limited. But no life is so limited in alternatives that it is not worthy of respect and entitled to safety and security against human abuses.

You are God's precious creation and God doesn't make junk. In the eventide, stroke yourself with acceptance, encouragement and emotional massaging.

Day 22:   A TROUBLED SEAT OF CONSCIENCE

Jumping to conclusions can be bad exercise. Proverb

As the saying goes, ninety percent of the time, we worry about things that only have a ten percent chance of happening. If the energy invested in worrying all across the earth were bottled and channeled into a productive outlet, only the imagination can fathom what the world would be like.

Disorganized ideas and uncertainty of outcomes contribute to the process of worrying. Science calls it "cognitive dissonance." Society calls it "stinkin' thinkin'." Either way, we have all employed illogical and half-baked thoughts which led to unnecessary dissention. Irrational opining can be harmful and negatively affect behavior.

The master artisans cradled a monastic attitude: to live a fulfilling calm existence—one free from commotion and unrest.

When engaging thoughts and tasks, begin deliberately with intent. Proceed at an even, stately pace and with wholehearted attention. That way, even the most arduous assignment may be accomplished leisurely with joy and for our own sake, not with worry and unfounded concerns.

The beliefs we formulate about events have a direct bearing on the outcome of any actions we take in the aftermath. If we are inaccurate in our appraisal of occurrences, the repercussions of how we handle situations will be amiss. We must confirm that our conclusions are levelheaded and honestly examine our mode of evaluation.

Listen before you leap. Ponder before you pounce. Analyze before you actualize. Reason before you rise. Communicate with God before you strategize an agenda. Pray that He may guide your course.

Once you have exorcised yourself of unsound and unreasonable thinking templates, when the vapor vanishes and the smoke clears, a new cognition will flow from within. Being able to manage internal tussles with diplomacy, your new parlance puts you in vogue.

Ultimately, may all you do become what you love. Co-create with the Chief Artisan in the grand plan of life.

Day 23:   STARTING OVER

If your dreams turn to dust ... vacuum. Proverb

Canton, Ohio, is the home to one of the nicest people I know, Frank. Living in a house adjacent to a quiet creek, camel-colored deer playfully meander in his backyard. Occasionally, an otter cruises downstream.

So what prompted frantic pounding on Frank's door in the middle of the night one spring?

The creek behind his house sporadically rises after heavy rains. It usually returns to normal within a few days. But that year, a startling about-face occurred. Flooding waters engulfed the entire lower level of the home along with its contents.

Asleep while the deluge ensued, a neighbor abruptly woke Frank from his slumber by banging on his door. As the storm devoured the first story, the two men posted on a dry windowsill until the Red Cross rescued them in a motorboat. I can't even surmise what must have been going through Frank's mind when he left everything to ruin. Many items lost held personal value and could never be replaced.

THE BUTTERFLY COMETH

If I had been there and had been granted a quick dash inside to retrieve just one item, I contemplated what I would have chosen.

Would it have been the new MP3 player my sister gave me for Christmas? How about my precious photo album holding all the great memories of my life? Or would I have latched onto my work diskettes which contained hours and hours of marketing presentations? The letters I accumulated over the years from the love of my life? What about my grandmother's wedding ring, a dear heirloom passed on from generation to generation? My late father's medal of valor?

What item would you choose?

Take your mind on an odyssey of what you embrace. Evaluate the importance of your choices. Prioritize what is significant to you and best for your life. If you are not happy with the rank of your assessment, construct a list of changes. It need not be accomplished overnight. Just make a list and let it simmer. Then hit the bed. Snuggle up with a good book and two down feather pillows. Delve into the luxurious world of literature. Have a ball. Tomorrow will take care of itself.

Day 24:   AWARENESS

We think in generalities, but we live in detail. Alfred North Whitehead

Which would you prefer: planting flowers in the warm pleasing aurora of daybreak or designing architectural plans in an air-conditioned office building?

Whether we consider ourselves as more "warm" or more "cool" is a personal self-concept of forming identity. From the earliest of times, man had a need to explain to himself the marvels of the world around him in terms of his own identity and contribution. For example, chronicles were invented to describe bread-making, cultivation of grain and harvesting a vintage to ferment wine.

The quest for this knowledge teaches us that we claim our real identity and our destiny when we seek to connect with our ancestral heritage. When you know your people, it is then that you discover who you are.

DIANA LOUISE WEBB

William Blevins advises that you have a personal responsibility to define yourself, not just with respect to your own being, but also in relation to your participation in the family system. Claiming responsibility, you outline your own ideals, values and behaviors rather than granting others the power to do so or allowing your environment to dictate your thoughts, beliefs and feelings. Systematic roles preserve uniqueness of the family unit. You have an individual character and a supporting part. These roles translate how families are organized and how they function. What affects one member affects all members.

There is a model of wholeness in the family—an emotionally close attachment and stability as well as cohesion in which one member "completes" the other members. Innate in that system, you have to have crafted your individual life and freely contribute the offerings of your authentic self.

Nineteenth-century philosopher, Soren Kierkegaard, conjectured that the deepest human despair occurs when choosing to be someone else rather than yourself.

Questions about personal identity never have uncomplicated answers because one comprises his or her life from a blend of factors, including genetics, culture, circumstances into which one was born, choices, geographical location, environmental considerations and the era in which one lives.

Whether you come from a big family or a small family, the family unit is more than the sum of each individual part. It is the spine of united energy. The fundamental variability within the literal meaning of "family" is contingent upon the enthusiasm the members are willing to invest in the kinship. A balance must be struck between individuality and togetherness.

Despite the scope to which your family unit inspires development, you are ultimately the one responsible for how you choose to acknowledge the family traditions, beliefs and values the members offer.

You have the final word on who you really are. Many elements sway us in determining what that statement means, but none more significant than an awareness of God. As long as we keep our bows rosined with the salves of His abode, then all of our personal characteristics including whether we possess a "warm" or "cool" personality type, will complete us.

Working overtime, our Creator stocks a cistern with sacred minerals and oils to supplant in untold millions the balm to make us whole. Basted, our Indiana Jones thirst for lost treasures will be quenched by Holy Titanium ore deposits along our shoreline. Lending in love, He is in us and we are in Him.

Our part: assert our right God's style.

... Then the world will know that you sent me and that you loved them just as much as you loved me. John 17:23

Day 25:   THE HOPE OF LIFE IN DEATH

It matters not how strait the gate, how charted with punishments the scroll, I am the master of my fate, I am the captain of my soul. William Ernest Henley

In my hometown, a man was accused of abandoning the farm animals in his barn after a flood. The ensuing heat compounded what was already a heartless act and the livestock died a miserable death.

The entire town expressed hatred for the man and the merciless act he committed. Usually crimes against children and animals are frowned upon far more than random victimless violations. But can we string someone up from the tallest tree because we hate him or her?

Somewhere in the core of the man who committed this cruel act is a worthy person. His worthiness was sequestered in a moment of horrible insensitivity and indifference for animal life. Be that as it may, we have to despise the sin, but love the sinner. In the very same way God's loving arms wrapped around the broken animals in an everlasting hug, God has a special place prepared for the perpetrator as well. That individual is the one who must accept the acquittal through repentance and move on to a new life—one where his sins have been absolved.

Eternal salvation cannot be better expressed than by Ellie Green who foretells, "We stand awed and dazed because we did nothing to earn it. Jesus simply loved us so much He gave us salvation so we could experience happiness forever."

As you stand in awe, graciously accept the gift.

No eye has seen, no ear has heard, and no mind has imagined what God has prepared for those who love Him. 1 Cor. 2:9

Day 26:   PHYSICAL WELLNESS

We know nothing of tomorrow. Our business is to be good and happy today. Sydney Smith

Physics, a riveting field of science, is the study of matter and energy. Matter is everything seen and unseen. It consists of limitless tiny particles called atoms. Matter takes the form of solids, liquids and gases. Ice is an example of a solid. When it melts, it turns into water, a liquid. When water is boiled, it becomes a steam, a gas.

Since liquids flow, they need something to keep them together. Scientists call the forces of attraction "cohesive forces." These forces interact with liquids to create surface tension.

We, too, have sampled surface tension. The biggest struggle is within ourselves. Searching for the ultimate pie in the sky, our slice of life is gorged with attaining immediate gratification. But more often than not, we mistake our concept of desire as God in the making while it is really superceding God. The earthly sweet tooth is yet another conceptualization of man's world which absorbs energy and causes stress. When we strive to free ourselves from this misconception, friction hatches. The combat will only be quieted by the pure delights given by the Lord.

When incomplete and ungratified, we pay tribute to the trickiest form of idolatry—self-hatred. Mechthild of Magdeburg elaborated on the theory of internal strife. The philosopher pegged self-hatred as being the worship of unrealistically high expectations of self. Those expectations justify the secret thrill of hating self when they are not met. The result: the infiltration of physical illness and infirmity. That is why God gives birth to Himself within us. He wants us to be fulfilled. We may then deflect all falsity and unwholesomeness. We cannot lose anything we have by way of birth. When the sacred excellence stirs our very core, we begin to notice changes in our approach to life. The desire to willfully sin departs from the battle zone. We are left at an armistice.

This truth regenerates a sense of satisfaction. Our good feeling casts outwardly to silhouette our physical wellness.

This day, profile pepped up health, fitness and invigoration.

Day 27:   COURAGE

A hero is no braver than an ordinary man, but he is braver five minutes longer. Ralph Waldo Emerson

It was to be the contract of the century. Reader's Digest called it "the biggest project since the pyramids." Dyed-in-the-wool cynics said it would never happen. But in the early 70s, two 110-story highrises opened their doors in New York City as the World Trade Center. The structures were breathtaking. From the observation deck of Tower Two, one could see forty-five miles in every direction.

In a shocking onslaught, on February 26, 1993, a rented van containing hydrogen canisters in the equivalent of ½-ton dynamite drove into the garage under the complex and exploded. Killing six people and injuring 1,042, the attack fared to be the worst terrorist act committed on American soil. However, the skyscrapers stood to reopen in less than one month.

Eight years later on September 11th, the World Trade Center's defenses were again penetrated. This time, the twin towers failed to survive a direct hit by two hijacked jetliners. The two-ton sky giants smashed into the central core traveling in excess of 400 mph. The infrastructure weakened, causing the collapse of both towers. Shortly thereafter, a sinister plot revealed two other carriers faced the same fate—a collision course with national landmarks.

It is horrifying to speculate what transpired in the minds of the passengers as well as in the minds of the occupants of the World Trade Center. Planes from United and American Airlines were involved in the heart-pounding fright. My sister was traveling on 9/11 on a United flight. By the grace of God, the aircraft on which she was flying was not the subject of terrorist activity. She learned the nauseating truth when the plane landed.

The dismay of how life can be easily extinguished is a startling wake-up call. In the twin towers disaster alone, nearly 3,000 people perished and approximately 343 firefighters didn't return at the end of the day. A member of the media reported how firefighters wrote their social security numbers on their arms prior to their rescue missions. This made identification possible should they have died in the line of duty.

It is impossible to conceive the wearisome relief crusades heaving heavy equipment and battling thick black smoke. The uncertainty of what the immediate future held had to consume everyone involved, but made no difference to these heroes. They were and are our security blankets and our knights in shining armor.

Inside of each one of us is a hero. That hero emerges and transcends in the same way God appears with his helicopter and rope. He may not be there when we want Him to be, but He is an "on-time" God. He instills courage which makes us stronger so in the most dismal of hours, we can go that extra heroic five minutes. When it appears God is no longer walking beside us, it is because He is carrying us.

As Jesus carries you, be an example of God's love in affirming His courage. Carry others in times of hopelessness, dejection and resignation.

Day 28:   TWO HEARTS THAT BEAT AS ONE

Someone once told me that not even for a million dollars would they touch a leper. I responded, "Neither would I. If it were a case of money, I would not even do it for two million. On the other hand, I do it gladly for the love of God." Mother Teresa

There is a saying which repeats itself throughout history: In life, you have two loves—your first love and your true love.

But first the love for self must be discovered as one cannot give what he or she does not hold. The French philosopher, Saint-Exupéry, quoted, "Perhaps love is the process of my leading you gently back to yourself." What he alluded to is the authentic self—the rebirth of the "true" you.

THE BUTTERFLY COMETH

Then when you meet a special someone who completes you, together, all the right stuff is there to embark on a journey which is to be the most fabulous expedition of your lives. The biggest problem is that two people approach relationships and marriage with a theoretic angle, the idea that falling in love is so that people can live happily ever after. When love is approached in that fashion, the fairytale shatters and couples divorce—seeking another fairytale elsewhere.

The idea of a fairytale is not completely erroneous, though. But that lifestyle does not come about magically. It comes by learning "the ropes." A couple's feet pattern must swing in sync with the song in their hearts. Critics find this analogy unrealistic, but if we don't create our own fairytale, who will?

Relationships are never perfect. They must start with a foundation. That foundation should be God. When He comes first, the union may bend and sway, but will never break. Why? Because each step of the way, through God, you strengthen one another. You then neither lose your savvy for laughter nor lose sight of the exciting feelings which brought you together because there is something solid to fall back on. Mistakes are made and things are not always smooth, but the tough times teach you how much love there is in pain and suffering. When one tumbles, the other is right there to pick up the pieces.

The worst blunder a couple makes is to take a partner for granted and devalue the "little things." Keeping the connection fresh and the lines of communication open cultivate the mutual respect, trust, intimacy and honesty to allow the marriage to thrive. The process leads you gently back to yourself, reinforcing the security of the relationship.

This evening, take your partner by the hand, cozy up on the couch and each of you make a list of the ten best qualities you value in the other. Share your lists. Take a moment to reminisce about the five best times of your lives together. Recall the laughs. Remember the first smiles. Strike an unsullied match to rekindle the spark in your eyes. Mix two scoops of rainbow sherbet with a pint of 7-UP in a blender. Slide in two straws. Cuddle up. Sip away!

Diana Louise Webb

Day 29:   FORTUNE

Knowing how to win is the first step. We must also know how to make use of our victories. Polybius

    Aspirin—the "cure all" wonder remedy which no contemporary medicine cabinet is without. More scientifically known as acetylsalicylic acid, aspirin came to us from Germany by the Bayer Drug Company in 1890. But the pain reliever dates back to the mid-1700s. In 1758, Edward Stone, an English clergyman, discovered that the bark of a willow tree he stumbled upon secreted a bitter sap. The chemical properties matched bark previously obtained in South America which had been used to reduce fever and treat malaria.

    Upon further testing of the newfound willow, it hailed remarkable success in decreasing high temperatures and soothing pain. What good fortune! However, the antidote didn't materialize until 1826, as Stone could not discern which part of the bark warehoused the active ingredient. For almost seventy-five years, the world missed out due to simple ignorance.

    In our own lives, how man times have we missed out because we were too dense or empty-headed? By holding on to rude awakenings, not accepting apologies and wailing in denial, we let "cure all" wonders slip on by. Akin to the bark of the willow undergoing a filtering process to generate the final product, we, too, can filter out impurities. The pain of recovery after swallowing our pride is never longer than necessary.

    Glistening with enlightenment, make your good fortune and wisdom available in the pharmaceutical coffer of life. That way, others may tap in as needed to share in a cornucopia of wonder.

Day 30:   CHERUBIM

Angels are the dispensers and administrators of the Divine beneficence toward us. John Calvin

    The circle of life is full of many dear people. In my circle is Sister Pat, a loving Catholic nun.

THE BUTTERFLY COMETH

One afternoon, after lunch, Sister Pat went to the bank to deposit a check. Prior to entering the institution, an acquaintance whom she had not seen for a long time stopped to chat. She wanted to continue the small talk, but needed to make a deposit before 1:00 p.m. to insure the transaction would be credited that day. With time short, a "little voice" prompted her to hurry off and take care of business.

About ten minutes after leaving the bank, sirens blared loudly and police cars swarmed the savings and loan: a robbery in progress.

Had Sister Pat prolonged her entry into the bank any longer, she would have been caught amidst a dangerous holdup. The "little voice" inside prodding her to hurry and take care of her business was that of a cherub.

Our angelic messengers protect us and guide us. Residing in cubbies watching for those moments of peril when they may be handy and of useful service, angels are the power of a higher presence. They are our patrons from the unseen.

From Angels, by Armand Eisen, "Angels appear, and in one way or another, help us, advise us, inspire us, or amaze us." Folklore proclaims that when a bell rings, an angel receives his wings. When the celestial being then flies down and kisses your heart, your own boulders and rubble burgeon wings and the baneful ebony flies away. Shadows infuse with lambent radiance. You live in the face of Jesus. It is an occasion for all seraphim to rejoice.

The root word for "rejoice" is "joy." J-O-Y can be translated into Jesus, Others and You.

1. Keep Jesus in the forefront.
2. Help others.
3. As the angels take care of you, take care of yourself. Feed your spiritual self and blossom.

In the daily swish of the celestial energies, recognize that your angels are there to veil you with a sheer pelisse of loving care and protection. Abide in the advice of St. Francis de Sales and "make friends with the angels who, though invisible, are always with you. Invoke them often and trust in their help and assistance in all your temporal and spiritual affairs."

DIANA LOUISE WEBB

As you weave your connection into life, know that your answer is leavened with a firm "yes" when someone asks if you have the joy of the angels in your heart.

Day 31:   CONTROL

We have it in our power to begin the world again. Thomas Paine

Would you ride a bicycle on a tightrope across Niagara Falls?

Probably not, but we don't really care if the next guy does it. In fact, we all got excited when the Great Wallendas did their high-wire acts. So what exactly are we, as humans, frightened for ourselves?

The explanation is very basic. Hedgehopping high above land lends itself to a total lack of control on the part of the traveler. Unable to bridle fate, in the event of a calamity, death is imminent. Bottom line: death scares us. If we were not afraid to die, we would not hesitate to walk on the wire.

So why are we apprehensive? The answer is two-fold: (1) We haven't done all we want to do on earth so we don't want to extinguish our future quite yet; and, (2) The Great Beyond is a total mystery. No one likes to come face-to-face with the unknown.

Death is unreckonable. We know neither the day nor the hour. God is the one who has blueprinted our life span. He is the Alpha and the Omega. His plan includes our conception and the time when we will breathe our last breath—an appointment no man may cancel.

During that cycle, our parents or caretakers nurture us. From their rearing, we develop our own franchise on life, establishing independence. While young, we are dependent. As we grow older, we become self-reliant. We are in control. We make choices. Whether poor ones or good ones, we are the decision-makers and there is considerable comfort in doing so.

But what happens when our reel breaks? Our presence is not doomed to anarchical failure. We each have a special assignment. We are the pencil. God is the lead which gives the pencil life. As long as we follow His teachings, our pencil will write and produce sweet marks. And it is not so much what we do as opposed to what we don't do that God will judge more harshly. When mankind acts or reacts, it is out of human weakness. God understands and tolerates weakness—more so than He tolerates not acknowledging human dignity.

<u>Violence of Love</u> author, Oscar Romero, ushers us to a road which lies from the ear to the heart that only God can travel. If our road is blocked by apathy and indifference to everyone but self, the beacons lit by our conscience get snuffed out in traffic and don't reach us. We then question how this behavior will be viewed in the afterlife and become afraid to die so we won't have to find out.

When you feel overcome by uneasiness brought about by lack of control, remember God is walking with you. In His wallet, your picture is right there. As He cradles you, cradle Him. When you put Christ first, He will let you in on what makes the sojourn on earth abounding.

<u>Day 32</u>:   TRANQUILITY

Quiet lives are like stones: They grow in the depths and no one knows anything about them. But sometime later the great cathedrals will be built from them. Ernst Wiechert

Within the serenity of our inner child, lives an extraordinary ladder to the fourth dimension. It is our imagination waiting to be unearthed from its peaceful existence. It rests on a mountain of grit. Doused with potential, this "sleeping giant" harbors the resoluteness to actualize grand undertakings. Not only is it creative, it is strong, capable and teeming with stamina.

Ernst Wiechert emphasizes to us in his own subtle way that it is o'kay for man to live a quiet and tranquil reality. In fact, it is more than o'kay. It is from the reserved that the brilliant and clever are born.

We are a society of thinkers, talkers and doers. The doers are the resourceful geniuses. They fine-tune their conventional skills to construct masterpieces. Each magnum opus unfolds from a thought by a quiet mind—an artist at work. The churning of ideas thrives in the privacy of the fourth dimension.

When the seat of consciousness calls, steep a hot cup of peppermint tea and employ the occasion to knock at the door of your fourth dimension. Do so in solitude. Luxuriate in a bath of creative juices. Plunge into the pool of visionary arts. Fantasize. Immerse yourself in mental gymnastics.

Taste tranquility.

Day 33:   SECOND CHANCES

The real fault is to have faults and not try to mend them. Confucius

The U.S. Holocaust Memorial Museum is home to a very significant commemorative dedication. It serves in memory of the 6,000,000 people who were put to death in gas chambers or died in concentration camps during Hitler's Nazi regime (1933-1945).

The Nazis came to power in 1933. Germany and its people had no idea what result the decimating outcome of the regime would bring. They endorsed policies without thinking.

When WWII broke out, times were extremely difficult. Germany collapsed in 1945 after it lost the war. With destruction great and malnutrition vast, a slow rebuilding process ensued.

During WWII, my grandfather fought in the German army against the Soviets at the Russian front. He had a scrape with the Nazi regime while making machine parts for the war effort in a large factory. One day before eating his lunch, he created a little jingle prayer in jest. In the company of his co-workers, he remarked:

Come Mr. Göbbels, be our guest
and give us what you promised us.
We don't want margarine or herring,
we want what you eat and Mr. Göring.

Dr. Joseph Göbbels was Hitler's Minister of Propaganda and Enlightenment. Through manipulation and distortion, he promised the German people victory. He promised them the good life. Of course, none of it ever materialized. Hermann Göring was the leader of the National Socialist Party in Hitler's government. Obviously, they both ate well and enjoyed a life of extravagance. Living in a dictatorship, no one was allowed to comment about Hitler and definitely not create political jokes.

THE BUTTERFLY COMETH

The next day after the incident, my grandfather was interrogated and his co-workers were questioned about his comments. A man subsequently showed up to work side-by-side with him under the auspices of being a new recruit. He was dressed in a brand new uniform. Everyone knew the man was a member of the Gestapo as no one could afford a new work uniform during such hard times. The man continuously made negative comments about Hitler in an effort to make my grandfather acquiesce which he did not do. Had he made a negative statement, he would have been led off to a concentration camp.

Joseph Göbbels committed suicide when the Soviet troops stormed Berlin on May 1, 1945.

Hermann Göring surrendered to American forces in 1945. He was charged at the Nuremberg Trials. After a verdict of guilty and being sentenced to death, Göring escaped a fate of hanging by poisoning himself.

I wonder if any of the individuals responsible for war crimes repented? Even now, we see the remembrances of how cruel humans can be to one another. Only when we recognize ourselves as sinners and honestly return to purifying and recharging ourselves are we able to be enlightened and helped by God. We can always have another chance. That's reality. Albert Einstein once said, "One cannot but be in awe when contemplating the mysteries of eternity, of life, of the marvelous structure of reality." When we turn away from the teachings of Jesus, His arms are still open. God is a God of "Second Chances."

Red-stained the clean white robe He wore,
as blood did spill from every pore.
Then with His arms still limp and weak,
did lift me up and kiss my cheek.
Through your repentance did He say,
your sins have now been washed away.

Day 34:   EVEN A BRICK WANTS TO BE SOMETHING

Only a mediocre person is always at his best. W. Somerset Maugham

Diana Louise Webb

It was the morning of November 4, 1922, in the Valley of the Kings on the Nile's west bank in Egypt. A water boy who was part of an archaeological team spear-headed by Howard Carter scooped out a handful of dirt for his water jug. By chance, he happened to step across the first step of Pharaoh Tutankhamun's tomb.

With further excavation, the steps formed a descending passage to a doorway. Behind the door, a chamber overflowing with golden artifacts of a vanished civilization surfaced. Almost 6,000 pieces were recovered.

Legend has it that a curse of untimely death would befall anyone who desecrated the grave. Giving credence to the theory, Englishman Lord Carnarvon, who financed the mission, died of a mosquito bite seven weeks after the coffin was opened.

As a cultured people, we request respect. But in order to get respect, we must give respect. To destroy, to ruin, to crush—these are all acts which quash reverential regard. What may seem to be insignificant still is a link in the chain of life.

God has handpicked each one of us to change the course of our previous generations if we elect to reside in Him. If we don't opt to follow Him, He will select another link during the course of time. It is by way of these developing generational personalities that an individual will be birthed to have the heart to follow God.

In the beginning of Earth's genesis, God created Eve to complete Adam. When Eve wasn't who she was supposed to be, she could never submit herself to God enough to shape Adam into who he needed to be. As the scenario replays itself daily in our current world, we are the ones equipped to make a difference—to "link up." If those around us continually emit bad seeds, then we adopt the same. The converse is also true.

Each step that framed the gallery to King Tut's mausoleum longed to be a "link" to magnificence. When the sarcophagus was defiled, it broke the chain.

There will always be a debate over whether exhuming relics of past civilizations is a principled action. What should not be in disagreement is that everything which works together to honor God and hallow His love deserves reverence. Splintering the links which join to fulfill God's master plan insults the fundamental human distinction of each component's deservedness to be something.

THE BUTTERFLY COMETH

We all want and merit being a link in the chain to greatness—even a brick wants to matter.

Day 35:   PURGING YOUR COMPUTER: THE PROCESS OF REBIRTH

We build more computers to hold more information, to produce more copies than ever, but we communicate less and less. George Carlin

My friend, Gerry, phoned me last week for advice about computers. Feverishly attempting to retrieve his hard drive which had crashed, Gerry was a wreck. He thought he could never recover or reorganize.

Our lives work like Gerry's computer. We thrust ourselves into overdrive and spread ourselves so thin that we cannot achieve our goals or take care of normal living tasks. Eventually, we, too, "crash."

Our society is one constantly "on the go." We do not promote "rest." But just as Gerry's computer needed a rest, to be cleaned out and files deleted, we, too, need to purge our own personal computers.

First, dust off your computer to rid yourself of stale thoughts and ideas. Refine the cleansing process by scouring between the keys and in small grooves to offer up a fresh crisp look.

Rearrange your base and keyboard to avoid becoming inactive and stuck in a routine. Add decorative garnish to treat yourself to a rare indulgence—a facial at a local spa, that chic sweater you've been scoping for several months or basketball tickets to a Bulls game.

Organize the inside of your computer. Create folders in which to store your general intellections. In each folder, categorize files to systematically arrange your beliefs.

Carefully examine your icons to take an inventory of your commitments and long- and short-term objectives. Access the chronology clock window to prioritize your time. Differentiate between necessities and wants.

Probe the "help" key to remind yourself that you can always reach out for love, that you are not alone and that God is only an e-mail away.

DIANA LOUISE WEBB

Flush out any old web sites which are lingering, but no longer productive and useful. This would include poor habits, blemished thinking and outdated technology.

Enter your recycle bin. Allow the experiences which may not have been positive, but a learning encounter, resonate so that future judgment errors may be minimized.

Surf the Internet to sharpen your skills and open your hibernating talents.

Update your software so that you may strive towards educational, spiritual and mental advancement. Modernize and renovate your hardware to maintain body fitness.

Explore the recreational computer disks of your soul. Take part in entertainment; thus, you don't become cemented. Click into the "Clip Art" so you never lose your flair for laughter.

Engage in one hour of manual research and write out notes in longhand to gain a renewed appreciation for your computer. Never abuse your system or take it for granted.

Finally, turn off your computer at the end of the day to give it a well-needed rest for a job well done.

Day 36:   PATRIOTISM

Do your duty and a little bit more, and the future will take care of itself. Andrew Carnegie

Washington, D.C. is a remarkable place to take a trip. Its magnetism and charm persuaded me as well. Enchanting advertisements landed my first-day itinerary on an outing to the Smithsonian Institute.

Immersed in historical culture, a gigantic American flag grabbed my attention. It measured 42 ft. x 36 ft. This banderole marked the original Star-Spangled Banner and emitted a stately aura of nationalism. Mary Young Pickersgill tailored the flag. She inherited the privilege as her mother constructed the first flag of the American Revolution. The commandant at Ft. McHenry enlisted Pickersgill to sew a banner "so large that the British will have no difficulty seeing it from a distance." One year later, it sparked a vision for Francis Scott Key to compose America's National Anthem. The Stars and

THE BUTTERFLY COMETH

Stripes will be forever and personify Woodrow Wilson's patriotic stance as "The emblem of our unity, our power, our thought and purpose as a nation."

That day, Old Glory beamed. It signified the same liberty and independence it did with its first wave. With rights come responsibilities. We, as citizens of this great nation, not only have a duty to ourselves, but also to our country. We must respect the ideals upon which America predicates itself. It is important to acknowledge that self-government does not give us the right to crush our neighbor.

Live each day responsibly. Be an example of John F. Kennedy's most notable and acclaimed slogan, "Ask not what your country can do for you, ask what you can do for your country."

Day 37:   TEMPTATION

In a moment of decision, the best thing to do is the right thing to do. The worst thing to do is nothing. Theodore Roosevelt

An Indian scripture puts into perspective the dichotomy surrounding gratification in man's world. The adage proclaims: Pleasure is one thing; wisdom is another. The first leads to sorrow, though pleasant at the time. The latter, though at first unpleasant, leads to lasting joy.

Temptation weaves itself into this quagmire. It announces a plethora of 'come hithers,' including affairs, coveting goods and rapacious acts. Comporting on impulse in response to a tempting stimulus, we fail to grasp the nucleus of who we are as children of God. Catching collective amnesia, we struggle with the flip side—who we are not. Led astray, we are ambushed. We won't be able to defy the evil if we don't put on the breaks.

Whatever temptation is being sent our way, God will give us the discipline of resistance, but we must adhere through "free will." We are God's people, but God never interferes with "free will." He gives us His hand to walk with Him, but He also lets us stray. That is the flavor of God's will: it is basically our will, but when it lends itself to a searing situation, God uses it for the greater good to make us more faithful. This discovery is not born in a laboratory; it is a living presence.

Diana Louise Webb

Close your eyes. Imagine stepping out of your body. Pick up a make-believe camcorder. Press "record" and execute a surveillance of your activities. Mentally rewind the video and play your "Day in the Life" movie. Are you proud of what you see? If not, don't allow man to snatch away your authority for change. Diving into the eye of vices severs the closeness to Christ's image. You are no longer recognizable—a washed out hologram. Until you can see from the outside in, you will continue to fall from grace.

As you probe life, live as if you would not be ashamed to have your "camera check" published on the front page of a major newspaper. Make your Kodak moment a blessed remembrance filtered by devout Christian principles

Day 38:   THE SWALLOWTAIL COMETH

Evil is a word we use when we give up trying to understand someone.
The Good Son

My final year of college, I toured a mental health facility during the spring semester of Child Psychology. The administrator, who provided an escorted visit, was in the process of transferring to another job. We spoke privately during a break and she verbalized that she felt useless at her position.

"I just can't reach the children. The acts they commit which result in being placed into our center are evil—plain evil, like setting fire to a church or throwing the family pet gerbil down a flight of stairs."

She further elaborated that the kids feel no remorse, citing, "You don't even see the regret."

As I walked through the various ward wings, a young boy named Gregory quickly volunteered to show me around. He couldn't have been more than twelve and seemed fascinated with the visitors. Greg grabbed my hand as if we had known each other for years. Together, we ambled through food service, a dayroom and then took a seat on the sundeck—an outdoor, upper patio enclosed in wire mesh. Greg brought a chair out for me along with a cold soda. He dusted off the top of the can with his shirtsleeve and clicked it open. Sitting on the concrete against the table edge, Greg quietly watched the clear sky.

THE BUTTERFLY COMETH

The temperate breeze created one of the nicest days of the month. I knew summer was almost here when several baby swallowtails fluttered with delight on the white picket fence.

Greg told me the reason he had been removed from his home was that he failed to show emotions. He misbehaved in his sixth grade class and his father repeatedly disciplined him with his belt. The bruises took their toll as the norm so he quit responding to life. Greg proudly admitted, "I never cried any tears."

At that moment, I felt hollow.

I explained to Greg that it was perfectly alright to cry and that tears didn't mean he was weak. In fact, in Barbara Johnson's book, I'm So Glad You Told Me What I Didn't Wanna Hear, Barbara pens, "Remember that the iron crown of suffering precedes the GOLDEN crown of glory. ...When God created you, He gave you emotions ... tears to help drain off the abscess of pain that's broken your heart. ... And when you cry, remember ... Jesus wept, too, when His heart was broken."

Unfortunately, boys are conditioned to be stoic and not sentimental, dictating, "It is not 'manly' to cry."

"I never said it wasn't o'kay to cry," purported Greg. "Just because you don't see the tears on the outside doesn't mean they aren't pouring down on the inside. For so long, my tears went unnoticed. Finally, they just dried up leaving an emptiness that nothing in this world can fill."

I immediately realized how misunderstood Greg was to his family and at the center. Even if the effects nullified, he just wanted attention to fill the void in his heart. The blankness made it unachievable for him to love or even "feel."

Make this a month to unseal your mind and heart to the pure expression of love and tolerance. Meet the breakthrough which merges the misunderstood with those who have given up understanding.

Day 39:   RISE UP IN GRACE

Be silent about great things; let them grow inside you. Baron Friedrich von Hugel

DIANA LOUISE WEBB

The Bugatti Veyron 16.4, topping out at a speed of 253 mph is one sleek flying machine. At that velocity, this turbo-charged super car could conceivably go airborne.

Have you wondered what it would be like to actually fly? Not in an airplane, not in a helicopter, not in a blimp—just simply being carried by the wind. This organic high is the perfect example of inner space exploration of the human spirit.

Patricia Hart Clifford touches the sphere of such a reconnaissance in her literary work, <u>Sitting Still</u>, reasoning, "Inner space holds a realm of existence not readily apparent when we are in the grip of the strident external world."

On that same echelon, Clifford shows us how to make the deeper travel. She proposes, "A powerful launching vehicle for the discovery of the realm within is silence. It is in the vessel of silence that inner transformation can occur."

We have an ache, an impulse inside, to ascend to the next level of life. This craving is not a contest. We are not competing to see who can make it atop the lotus land and then watch the masses sweat and toil below. The aim is ascertaining our highest dream in unification with the mind of our Creator. In stillness, by subtle absorption, we osmotically take in the nature of Christ.

On this newborn day, open your eyes, rise up and walk—just like He did.

Day 40:   VICTORY TODAY IS MINE

Nothing comes to sleepers but a dream. Lowell Fulson

Helen Keller, both deaf and blind, exemplified unprecedented successes not only in her own accomplishments, but also in the education of the handicapped.

Helen lived a precious life. She based her being on the principle that our existence is a sequence of teachings that must be lived to be appreciated. With each lesson is born a constructive gain which makes us first-class people.

We either learn by a sip or a gulp. Either way, we swim the sea one heartbeat at a time. We sink the same way or via a merciless plunge. The choice is ours whether we get back onto the water access to complete the race or whether we don't.

During this swim, we meet a lot of folks. Some freestyle with us and are there with a soothing liniment when we graze a sandbar or slam into a ridge. For those who leave complimentary impressions upon us, we feel the honey of their spirits spin into taffy in our hearts. We also cross paths with characters who shove us into blustery currents.

Remind yourself that the state of your water doesn't impede the victory. You may always surface to breathe in God.

Forever, victory is mine.

Day 41:   FOR THE LOVE OF A FATHER

There is always plenty of time, if you don't hurry. Rosie Schaap, <u>Guideposts</u>

My father was a terrific gardener. As a child, our home displayed a remarkable floral dress in the toasty summer months. My dad lovingly planted each bulb, delicately making sure not to mar any of the seedlings or shoots.

Bordering the iridescent wonderland, robust vegetables spanned the plot. A green patchwork quilt of lettuce, peas, onions, tomatoes, carrots, potatoes and turnips flourished in my father's care. I loved the good things to eat, but I never took time to learn the hobby. In fact, I didn't spend much time with my father. More important activities preempted: shopping with friends, listening to the radio and watching television. My father and I loved each other; we just didn't spend many quality moments together. I put those off for tomorrow—a tomorrow which never seemed to come. With each passing season, we each grew older. I can't remember where the years went.

In 1991, I graduated from law school. No one could have been prouder than my father. The day of the commencement ceremony, my mother hemmed his pants and got everything ready for the big affair. Twenty-two at the time, my future gleamed. So you can imagine how heartsick I was when my father suddenly took ill and couldn't attend the ceremony. Within two months, his health worsened. He was admitted into the hospital in Kansas City the day before I was scheduled for a job interview. That evening, I visited my father in the ICU. When I left, our eyes met and I whispered, "I love you, dad." Little did I know that this moment would be the last time I saw my father alive.

The next day after my interview, I drove to the hospital only to pass my mother and sister on the highway heading in the opposite direction. I turned around and followed them perplexed that they were not at the hospital. My mother appeared to be driving towards my apartment. Indeed, that is where we both finally parked. Crying when she opened the door, I knew instantly. My father was dead.

My mother told me they had arrived at the hospital a few minutes after a massive heart attack claimed dad's life. The nurses said when he took his last breath of life, a smile danced across his face. He was at peace. He was with God.

As I reflect upon the years that I was privileged to have my father, I regret I did not learn more from him; that I gave up irreplaceable times in order to keep a date with the mall, the radio, or the T.V. As humans, we seldom comprehend our regrets in time to rectify them. Obviously, they would not be regrets had we made corrections on time.

Dads are very special people—so extraordinary that the third Sunday in June is set aside every year to honor them. Dubbed "Father's Day," this celebrated holiday was signed into law by President Nixon in 1972.

There are those people for whom Father's Day does not bring cheer. A root of bitterness may have grown from a planted seed of a father not being there. This could be the result of an estrangement caused by alcoholism, abuse or years of denial or unrealistic demands or belittlement. But that doesn't mean there is no reason to celebrate. We are a part of two kinds of families: the one to which we are born and the one we make. We must not allow ourselves to be dragged down by either. We can maneuver beyond the earthly composition of the world to a Father at the center of all things.

This Father is someone who wants to spend more time with us than we with Him. This Father always forgives us and He does it out of love, never postscripting the condition, "I'll forgive you if…". He never demands anything, yet most of us only call upon Him when we want something. He is regularly available for conversation, but we usually choose to converse with someone else. Who is He who is so faithful?

He is our Father in Heaven who unconditionally loves us. When we pour ourselves out to Him, we cannot be defeated.

At the close of each day, celebrate your Heavenly Father. Thank Him for the generosity, joy and kindness of life. Thank Him for keeping you safe, for a healthy body and mind and for your daily bread. Finally, thank Him for His support and guidance as your loving Father—a relationship which completes the beauty God implanted in each soul.

You are loved. Pass it forward.

Day 42:   DIVINE LOVE

Any fact facing us is not as important as our attitude toward it, for that determines our success or failure. Norman Vincent Peale

Charles Lamb, an English author (1775-1834), claimed his fame through his outstanding essays and unique literary criticism. Reflected in his writings, Lamb's gentleness for humanity created quite a topic for fireside conversations.

He lived his life as the demeanor of his name, Lamb. In all of his ventures, he remained intimate with the sun, the breeze, greenery and candlelight. He delved into the remotest of reality. Bringing out the prime in the book-loving arts, the facemask of traditional scholarly works shattered and purity whisked through as Lamb calibrated the various loose sallies he penned.

Divine love does the same for mankind as Lamb accomplished for the world of writing. Riso and Hudson in <u>The Wisdom of the Enneagram</u> describe this concept. Divine love expresses itself as a powerful force that breaks all the old palisades and is just that: Divine love. It needs no introduction, no standing ovation, no compensation and no reward. It stands alone—a forever pathway to a light that never darkens.

Cast your net with love and a clear conscience, and you, too, will reap the free incentives. Your soul will direct your leaps. The e-train will take you on a straight trajectory allowing your spirit to wheel.

Diana Louise Webb

It's time to burst out of this world!

Day 43:   HUMILIATION

Not so much brain as earwax. William Shakespeare

At an office party, Josh, the nine-year-old son of my boss, pulled me into the hallway to whisper a secret.
"My best friend is Toby. His sister, Darcy, just won a marathon."
"Wow, how impressive!" I exclaimed.
Toby, also age nine, was at the party with his parents. Darcy couldn't come. Approximately fifty employees and their families attended the gala. Josh asked me to congratulate Toby on behalf of his sister and inquire how fast she could run. Of course, I accommodated the request and strolled over to the children's room packed with kids and parents.
In a loud bellow, sporting a huge grin, I spouted off, "So, Toby, how fast can your sister run?"
Dead silence fell.
Toby quietly put his hands in his pockets. Shifting is eyes to the floor, he murmured, "My sister can't run. She doesn't have any legs."
Unable to locate a piece of furniture under which I could fit, I gasped in total shock. Frozen in gross humiliation, I caught a glimpse of Josh smirking in the corner. Rage enveloped every cell of my body as I tried to slink away unnoticed.
When humiliated, the tendency is to become introverted and solemnly escape the situation or lash out in anger. To conquer humiliation, you have to regain control of your reactions. Concentrate on facing an uncomfortable situation head-on. There will never be recovery until you confront the drama. By not working through a mortifying incident, the healing process cannot begin.
The next time you take a tumble in a humiliating circumstance, catch yourself before you fall. Tactfully attain balance. Boot the furniture to the side as crawling under couches is no longer in your league.
Go forth in confidence!

THE BUTTERFLY COMETH

Day 44:   MOTIVATION

Don't wait for your ship to come in, swim to it. Proverb

In Montgomery, Alabama, on December 1, 1955, on a crowded bus sat Rosa Parks, an African-American seamstress and housekeeper, along with three other passengers of color. The bus driver, James F. Blake, requested the commuters to move so a white man could sit down. Parks refused to give up her seat, gaining momentum for the modern civil rights movement.

Subsequently arrested and assessed a $14.00 fine, the action spawned a series of boycotts which led to litigation. The Halls of Justice rocked when the Supreme Court overrode segregation ruling it unconstitutional.

Sooner or later, we learn to stand on our own. Within self-reliance, a realization of autonomy is sparked. We prepare our own ground to plant our seeds. We hoe, till, weed, fertilize and water. We then reap what we sow. Inherent in the process, we look for guidance. George Bernard Shaw elucidates that our garden is "The best place to seek God ... you can dig for Him there." When we do, we cross a motley of vantage points that qualify us to re-evaluate who we are. We recall from where we came. We reason for what we stand. We compute where we are going. We define our atlas. We map out a direction and scout the highways that we must drive to make munching the peach possible. We become our own initiative propelled by personal pyrotechnics.

Remember Thomas Carlyle's noteworthy shibboleth, "Life is a little gleam of time between two eternities." Live yours with passion and vitality. Know that the world is a better place because you are commissioned as the catalyst to make a difference.

Affirmation of the hour: Yes, I will!

Day 45:   RUNNING AGAINST THE WIND

The line between the end and the beginning is sometimes hard to discern, like the line separating the sand from the sea. They seem to run together for awhile and what we think is an ending often becomes a new beginning. Bill Gaither

Diana Louise Webb

We have all been there, but we would rather forget we have. The experience: our love tank running on empty. It commences when we are at the height of life. Living in the land of milk and honey, we are immersed in tremendous joy on a personal level, home and at work. Then, suddenly, we taste the steps of the runner's block and flee or are the ones left behind to scour the burnt rubber. The love tank went bankrupt. Why? Because we allowed fear to deplete our resources.

Every day, events occur which we keep to ourselves and do not share forthright with a companion, family member, friend or employer. They may include the effects of a traumatic breakup, the loss of a loved one, an unwanted pregnancy, incest, abuse, chemical dependency or grave illness. We try to overcome, but we have not been able to effectively implement the process because we can't quite put our foot forward. Immobilized, our spirit dies; our soul dies.

When we are swathed in the plushness of cashmere, we feel safe and comforted. Our cashmere is the security from our higher power. Without it, out of fear that our utter bliss will be ripped out from under us, we take off running. And how often does this happen—the "sure thing" ripped out from under us? The answer: plenty.

In the middle of such a letdown, Nityananda imparts an alternative remedy: "The heart is the hub of all sacred places. Go there and roam in it."

When all seems lost, we may rely on the heart that serves with an unending wellspring of living water not available through any "sure thing." The heart never fails us, as it is the center of love and goodness. When love saturates the corm of being, our basic vitals do not come from external means. They come by what God says to us and through our lives. We are rejuvenated by love to the realness of ourselves—sustaining us, healing us and encouraging us so that we may hold our own, stay afloat and survive any brouhaha.

However, most of us don't follow this. We refuse to risk the chance of abandonment and pain. The starting gate opens ... and off we go! Away we bolt via a lame excuse or maybe no excuse at all. We even secretly hope we can take the easy way out and drive the object of our love or good fortune to pull away from us so we won't have to pull away ourselves. In our view, it is better to not feel at all than to chance joy crumbling. We no longer want to hurt. At the slightest inkling that life is too good to be true, we make a swift getaway.

THE BUTTERFLY COMETH

What we have forgotten is that those from whom we are absconding are actually faithful stewards who are standing with open arms to replenish our hearts and spirits. These are our soul mates, our family members, our friends, our employers or our neighbors. They sire rays of sunshine and journey with us to brighten our world. They are there to hold us in their arms, calm our fears, boost our courage and enhance our self-esteem. Ready, willing and able, they always pick up the pieces of our brokenness. With Elmer's glue in hand, fragment by fragment, they repair us. Unfortunately, they can't do it without a chance—without our opening up.

Don't lose out on filling the heart's immortal carafe with the elation of emotion. Don't rob your love tank by blocking off the flow of love, happiness and what Plato referred to as "natural wealth"—contentment.

The next time you yearn to go on the lam, grab the hand of a friend or soul mate or confidant, and invite him or her on your wayfaring. Together, unseal your reservoir of anxiety, distress and fear. Open and explore the boxed trunk with a plan to lift your uneasiness and apprehension. Share hand-in-hand. Replace misgivings with faith, with a chance, with healthy vulnerability. The results will be mesmerizing. Then as your shawl of cashmere gently shrouds the two of you, embark on a race to follow the glacier to living water. As you hike in unison up and down the mountains of ice, heed the advice of William Inge and "never pay interest on trouble before it becomes due."

You are truly loved unconditionally and cherished. You are protected in the adoring hands and hearts of the people who find you simply amazing. Feeling the flow, your need to speed through life all alone dissipates.

No matter what bankruptcies you have endured, you are now living life. Love every minute of it!

<u>Day 46</u>:   AN EVENING AT THE POST

Don't take for granted precious gifts from above. Or lose sight of what means the most—a child ... a life ... a love ... In loving memory of Michelle Morgan

Diana Louise Webb

In 1916, a seventeen-year-old young man with a dream sold his first artistic magazine cover to The Saturday Evening Post. This U.S. illustrator was so well received that his artwork continued to be prominently displayed on the front cover of the publication for the next forty-seven years, a total of 317 magazine covers. His name: Norman Rockwell.

Depicting realistic detail, Rockwell's subjects were taken from everyday family scenarios adding in a touch of humor. His drawings peeped everything from neighbors helping neighbors to students studying lessons in a schoolhouse—all portraying grassroots America.

Rockwell died in 1978 at the age of eighty-four, leaving a legacy of simple-hearted joy and innocence.

My friend's friend, Linda, helped out at The Saturday Evening Post. She spoke of the journal as one that promoted the ideals by which Rockwell himself, firmly stood. By reminding society about the normal places and people we know and love, the magazine instilled in us that innocence is an enrichment which should be allowed to logically develop and that youngsters be allowed to grow up and that the world be allowed to continue to be the world.

The Post personified classic American life. Readers gravitated to the appealing themes and, like clockwork, read each weekly issue as part of their good 'ole down-home living.

In our life regimen, there are important things for which we, too, should set aside time. One of these things is prayer. Just as The Post brought delight in its own private setting to readers, prayer is worthy of its own time and place.

Whether early morning or into the late hours of the evening, prayer is a way to communicate with God in a meaningful way. Prayer fosters openness to God's presence, renders healing and quiets the soul. It provides an opportunity to show gratitude and praise. It lends focus to our spiritual inquiry.

Prayer involves adoration—a dependency upon Him to whom we direct our prayer. When praying, we must have faith in God and in His being the rewarder of those earnestly seeking Him (Heb. 11:6). When laid to rest six feet under, it is too late.

It is before the final analysis that you must approach God in the full assurance of faith seeking to abide in Him through prayer. As

THE BUTTERFLY COMETH

His child, you will inherit His will, including the teachings of His Son and His disciples.

How do you spend your evenings at life's post?

Day 47:   PATIENCE

When the occasion is piled high with difficulty, that's when we must rise with the occasion. Abraham Lincoln

When I was twelve years old, I used to babysit for a lovely family with five children—the youngest, an adorable four-year-old boy named Preston. One Friday night, I was upstairs preparing dinner when a loud crash vibrated from one side of the basement to the other. I dashed downstairs only to find Preston holding a golf club amid broken glass and smoke from a small television set. All that remained was a pile of inoperative electronic parts. Preston had knocked the TV off its stand. It crashed to the ground.

Preston looked up at me with one tear streaming down his check, "I was trying to kill a wasp on the TV show."

I bent down and gently wiped Preston's face.

"Why are you crying?" I inquired.

"Because he got away," he answered.

Children refresh us to the beauty and fulfillment of the fruits of the spirit: love, joy, long-suffering, peace, gentleness, goodness and faith. Hence, we must exercise patience with a will geared toward piety.

As quickly as the television was damaged, we, too, become damaged without prediction. Life is not always the lovely attraction portrayed in the movies.

The reasoning behind the lunacy can be just as convoluted. Our own lives simulate the methodology of Preston's smashing the television and his subsequent tears for missing the wasp. Patience soothes what is not congruent.

As a solution slowly unravels, we realize that which does not kill us will at least put off the inevitable until God's perfect timing manifests itself. As we tame the fervor within, we are resolved under both convenient and inconvenient circumstances. We uncover the best in ourselves and attach meaningful significance to God's graces. As insight is shed, we live a more fertile existence.

Tonight, share a story with a friend as to how one of the fruits of the spirits has touched your life. Discuss how you blessed someone else. As the two of you engage in dialog, abide in holiness and reverence.

Day 48:   EUPHORIA

You're supposed to enjoy every sandwich. Warren Zevon

Birth is one of the most glorious events in life. A tiny baby comes into the world—ten precious fingers and toes, soft hair, a button nose and captivating eyes. Yes, a celebration is definitely in order! People across the world express merriment in a variety of ways to observe birthdays.

The birthday cake, a treat without which no gala fiesta is complete, has its origin with the Greek goddess, Artemis. Legend has it that moon-shaped honey cakes topped with candles highlighted her big bash and spurred a tradition which has been handed down from generation to generation over the centuries.

Take this time to reminisce about the best birthday jubilee you celebrated. Everyone has a favorite. Recall the feelings of that special day. Relive the moment. Arthur Schopenhauer spawned the phrase, "Each day is a tiny life." Give that life a birthday rumpus. Do so with the same finesse and honor that you would lavish upon a newborn.

Bake a cake and have a shindig!

Day 49:   THE SAXOPHONE

Music attracts the angels in the universe. Bob Dylan

"As I passed the tall spruce," recaps Joyce Rupp in Out of the Ordinary, "it suddenly came alive with song."

Rupp's interpretation reveals the extent to which music offers itself as a poetic language of the soul. Continuing, "Deep inside the thickly branched tree the sparrows had been awakened by some inner alarm clock and began heralding the dawn with their symphony cheeps, quickly filling the gray day with the sparkle of their voices. I stood there amazed, my heart transformed. A smile came as I pondered that usually silent tree now filled with hidden music."

I, myself, delighted in a similar magnetism while passing a park bench in Philadelphia. An elderly man greeted tourists with a saxophone in celestial song—tunes so compelling that even the pigeons sprouted untrodden wings of harmonic peace. Every sound, every musical note, lifted me to a heightened level. It stimulated all that was tired, all that was dead.

We each hold an original song of the soul—a conversation between self and God. We play the instrument. We may either do so harmoniously or blindly hit the keys. Ergo, we create our own music to which we dance.

Sometimes we dance alone, such as the Mirange. Sometimes we dance as two, like the Tango. Sometimes we dance in lines, hip-hopping to the Electric Slide. Sometimes we dance in groups, as in the Square Dance. Regardless of how we dance, each day we learn a new stride.

As you begin this morning, make every step and note count. Find contentment in each overture. Be happy with your signature song. It is your life. Be happy.

<u>Day 50</u>:   CO-DEPENDENCY

This above all, to thine own self be true. William Shakespeare

The importance of identity and the many ways it affects our existence spill into all facets of life. It is crucial to establish an identity separate from that of our parents, siblings and friends. Also essential is to set boundaries so that we do not become so wrapped up in another person that we lose ourselves. Hence, the definition of co-dependency: our need to be needed spins out of control.

Since we co-exist with other people, mutual integrity and respect become integral components in relationships and friendships. This centers on the parties' encouragement of personal growth with one another. If this doesn't happen, we lose our identity and open ourselves to becoming co-dependent. We fall victim to low self-esteem and low self-worth.

Co-dependent people allow themselves to be invaded. They constantly put others first—their needs, wants and desires. The co-dependent vicariously live their lives through the reliance of someone else to provide feelings for them. This type of life sentence culminates into an emotional death penalty.

If that occurs, we are stunted in a time warp because we are not free. By our own binding leg irons, we fail to evoke our authenticity. To reclaim dominion, develop an inspired strategy. Siege the garrison of life, rescue the imprisoned spirit, slay the dragon and emerge victoriously by invoking self-acceptance. Once we can and are willing to accept ourselves, we are more on target and formulate a compassionate self-evaluation.

Positive self-talk is influential at this juncture to improve self-esteem. Breaking the breastplate which restricts and confines shows us that we have worth. Receptive to feeling our own emotions and thinking our own thoughts, we may then conclude that the only entity over which we have control is self.

Utilize this month to set new boundaries. Be assertive. Know that it is perfectly natural to have your own thoughts and opinions and to befittingly express them. Of utmost importance, love out of a pure heart, not because you feel a duty or compulsory obligation.

Day 51:   ORIGINALITY

One doesn't discover new lands without consenting to lose sight of the shore. Gide

A freezing winter weekend at a mock trial practice, one of the volunteers asked me if I would enjoy co-hosting a boxing match in Reno with a famous TV personality. It was a hypothetical question, but I gave it a considerable amount of thought. Imagine ... being in front of thousands of people at a hotel—live.

"Good evening, ladies and gentlemen. Welcome!" The applause thundering.

A wonderful icebreaker, the inquiry promised an interesting topic of conversation. An emcee can make or break the show.

THE BUTTERFLY COMETH

In our personal lives, our "emcee" performs the same function. Therefore, we need to enlist our minds to take on the role of a fanciful wizard. Creativity is a living bloodhound, not a stationary monument preserved in a museum. Only when we mine the well of originality in our own lives can it transverse outwardly.

Our innovative side sometimes chokes. Outside forces sway the way we think and stifle and distract us from unearthing the visionary within. In life, emphasis is placed on practicality as opposed to artistic ingenuity. We eat microwaved meals from paper boxes. We look for expeditious solutions to personal problems which doctor symptoms, but seldom cure the underlying quandary. We work for companies that operate on a consumer-need basis producing functional products instantaneously as cheaply as possible. Although this reasoning is not completely flawed, we should never be so honed in on the pragmatic that we forget the spirited energy coursing inside.

Let hopeful inventive resourcefulness see you through. Be a believer. The possibilities are endless.

<u>Day 52</u>:   THE GIFT OFFERING

No one can give you wisdom. You must discover it for yourself, on the journey through life, which no one can take for you. Sun Bear

When we look around at our present civilization, we stand in awe at the excellence of craftsmanship by our Maker. Accordingly, our curiosity is piqued as to what mental image of ourselves we will leave upon the human race when we depart. What tidbit of us will remain to be shared?

Kate, a girl I worked with at a restaurant years ago, and I frequented a cemetery in the old Midwest town of Hannibal, Missouri. The secrets hidden away on the memorial grounds absorbed our very souls as we squatted Indian style among the grave plots. Gracing the land, each grave tendered a final message via an imprint on its commemorative marker.

One particular headstone captured my attention. It was that of a woman born in 1899. She lived for only a mere thirty-five years. Her epitaph read, "Now she will waltz." My guess was that this individual must have led a grief-stricken life. Searching for solitude among the crowdedness of all that plagued her, she was finally free.

Another square-shaped marble marker belonged to a man who died in 1780. "Liberty's source is God" faintly shadowed the trite sculpture. This person's life obviously mingled with the ideas promulgated in the Declaration of Independence.

Granted that all the inscriptions differed, one commonality evidenced itself: a need to bid adieu with a legacy by which to be remembered.

Kate asked me what I would choose to have engraved as my epitaph. She expressed hers would bear the slogan, "A light in a dark world." I think mine would simply state, "She moved with the cheese."

What parting words would you like voiced on your tombstone when it's time to say sayonara to the earth?

The irony is that this "goodbye" is really not "goodbye." The last chapter of your book is a beginning—a time when the gap between the Alpha and the Omega is united and the realistic recognition of how well you loved in this life unveils itself. What you own, the titles you hold, the cars you drive and the plush careers you embrace will carry no significance. The deposits in your savings account that you will take with you are not Benjamins or stock certificates. They are the fond reminiscence that roses really do bloom abundantly in winter.

As you rise through your outer coverings, your arguments, obsession with self-importance, vanity, yokes you lug around and money to which you lay claim, will be left behind. That baggage is meaningless. What does matter is how you labored in the vineyard of the purpose for which you were created and whether you believed the sacrifice at Calvary was good enough.

This day, as you wake, remember that all you have to do is be your authentic self. God made you out of love to love. Within this sacred reverence, you will come to know one truth, one body.

Then when you give that final wave of sayonara to the earth, you will have discovered the secret of why the only life worth living is a principled one.

Delight in the vision that the best is yet to come.

Every part of nature teaches that the passing away of one life is the making room for another. The oak dies down to the ground, leaving within its rind a rich virgin mould, which will impart a vigorous life to an infant forest. The pine leaves a sandy and sterile soil, the harder woods a strong and fruitful mould.

So this constant abrasion and decay makes the soil of our future growth. As I live now so shall I reap. If I grow pines and birches, my virgin mould will not sustain the oak; but pines and birches or perchance, weeds and brambles, will constitute my second growth.

Henry David Thoreau
October 24, 1837

THE QUEST FOR MORE
FROM THE BOTANICAL GARDENS IN RIO DE JANEIRO, BRAZIL

In life, we reach a point where we hunger for a face-lift. Whether it is a makeover of the heart or one of the flesh, we yearn for virtue, beauty, knowledge and happiness.

On this sally, Christel unfolds her wings and indulges in a jaunt to the botanical gardens of Rio de Janeiro. Brazilian floriculture advances opulence comparable in kind to the glorious florets of a successful, hopeful, possible and spectacular life.

Join Christel in nourishing your inner garden. Uncover simple enjoyment in abundance. Unmask the ivy vines that shadow the Simon-pure you. Engage the truth of the rose bush. Lose your consummation of the speckled thorns of the cactus plant. Get rid of your overgrown busyness.

This season: Flourish in colorful landscaping.

Day 53:   SNOW-IN-SUMMER

Life is a glorious banquet, a limitless and delicious buffet. Maya Angelou

Metaphorically representing a blanket of snow, the snow-in-summer plant is a gorgeous mass of white flowers and fanciful stems—suiting the most finicky of tastes. In literal terms, when we speak of "snow in summer," we visualize a damper on life. But with the right attitude, we will never have to see snow in summer. Why? Because when we hula the "bad breaks," we live in an armistice of well-being which allows us to thaw ourselves in the opulence of sunshine.

In order to defrost, we cannot do it solo. We need a pilot light. And as long as we keep it lit, we hold the reconditioning necessary to make the mental adjustments to meet life's ultimatums. That passion inside is Jesus Christ and the operative declaration that galvanizes our tin is "I can do all things through Christ which strengtheneth me" (Philippians 4:13). With God, nothing is impossible.

Just when we think it is going to snow on our sunny backyard barbecue, our snow blower's autopilot ignition spontaneously clicks into action. Within minutes, it presses forward at full tilt velocity to redirect the delicate flurries. With sacred energy, we recoup our rays. We adapt to new beliefs. Only when we remodel our attitude and release ourselves from narcissism do we find that it truly does not snow in summer.

What we experience is the love of life. Not only is our barbecue sans blizzard, the sun is also shining. We feel a little touch of Heaven—part of the magic of the unknown which completes the crown of the flesh and blood.

Day 54:   LEMON BOTTLEBRUSH

Unhappiness is not knowing what we want and killing ourselves to get it. Don Harold

A fast-growing shrub, the lemon bottlebrush's trademark is its many-stamened red flowers which resemble bottlebrushes. For me, the term "bottlebrush" brings to mind a Victorian dungeon scene packed full of serfs scouring mason jars the old-fashioned way.

An unappealing chore, cleaning usually takes a backseat to more attractive options. After all, what could be any less exciting than rummaging through dusty boxes in an attic and throwing out years of

THE BUTTERFLY COMETH

build-up? In our efforts to clean up the rooms in our home, how often do we think about cleaning out the rooms where it really counts? Laundering our personal attic ranks lowest on the procrastination list.

Perhaps instead of rehashing and storing, it is time to remember and then to let go. Whenever we explore our past, there is a need, a reason. When we resist acknowledging difficult issues and stash them away, we are not dealing with the drama. Growing up in denial makes it easy to live in denial. By not reaching genuine feelings, we are never whole. Thus, we cannot acquire peace of mind. With something missing, we seek out paste to bind together our private awful secrets and losses, leaving a gaping hole which we attempt to shield with a tarp. This wet, transparent blanket, riddled and torn, makes a poor showing for a cover-up. Unable to bridge the difference between fantasy and reality, we are hijacked.

But no rift is without a ramp. When things in the attic haunt life, the cause is supernatural, not psychological. We must then believe or not believe in God. In <u>The Will to Believe</u> by William James, James weighs the gain and losses if we stake all on God's existence: "If you win in such case, you gain eternal beatitude, if you lose, you lose nothing at all."

In believing, you merge with a restorative and peace-making force. For a believer, this loving power faithfully serves happiness. At the end of the day, can you say the same?

<u>Day 55</u>:   HYBRID TEA ROSES

They had discovered the value of a little time and love between best friends. Gary K. Farlow

At the onset of summer, as we sample the sweet redolence of roses, we note the fullness of their interlocking branches. We, too, link up with exceptional peers who touch our inner being like no others. These precious individuals are our friends whom we should embrace.

A friendship needs to be nurtured. Like the rosebush, when watered and showered with sunbeams, it blossoms into a spectacular conglomerate. A friendship's strong stem signals its internal stability. The thorns metamorphose before our very eyes into unique and angelic instruments which form healthy boundaries. Each petal is extraordinary, representing an assortment of talents offered freely. The center core reinforces wisdom—the progeny from which we derive advice. The ornate leaves grasp the pedicel between the thorns as a constant reminder that a friendship toils troubled waters and stands strong in the face of adversity.

Our friends wrap us with love and devotion. We make them the lead in our play and hang a star on their dressing room door. We create a backdrop of regal canvas plaited into a dossal of endearment, understanding and loyalty.

On opening night, salute your friends with a dozen yellow roses—lest you never forget the warmth and kindness of those who ease your cares, increase your joy, comfort your sadness and share in your accomplishments.

Day 56:   DUTCHMAN'S-BREECHES

Hey, it's OK ... if you're not exactly conquering the world, professionally. To somebody out there you're a VIP—no matter how tiny your paycheck, Rolodex or office space. Alexandra Marshall

The Dutchman's-breeches, so-named for the semblance of rows of miniature trouser flowers, is confirmation that every living creature wears pants and puts them on one leg at a time.

Created equal, we are one nation under God. We, as God's people, have a special place in this world in association with one another. We are all mothers, daughters, fathers, sons, sisters, brothers, aunts and uncles. We depend on others and others depend on us. Our interdependent bonds give us a sense of belonging which is necessary to relate to our surroundings from a self frame of reference.

The best we can give to mankind is a well-rounded and happy person. How we flourish comes from within and is not contingent on foreign forces. Therefore, the more we give, the happier we are.

When we utter rasping words, gossip at the office water fountain, give a stony and unapproachable glare, or disparage another's reputation, we are pointing a finger in judgment. For every "one" finger we point at others, three are aimed back at us.

THE BUTTERFLY COMETH

Mart De Haan wrote about how God admonishes us that if we write off what it is like to be at the bottom, we are no longer fit to be on top. By adopting a "holier than thou" air of superiority, we ignore God's almighty power in spurring our recollection that no one can don the pant leg better than the next fellow.

When we reach the point where we think we are "above" it all, we need to open the drapes and let life in. Look at other people the way Jesus does. Being contoured every second, we may either migrate in the direction of His image or we may move away from God's plans. Treating those around us nicely and with humility opens the door wider and wider to a better fit for life.

We each put our pants on one leg at a time. What differentiates us from one another is how well we love and the way we love.

Could you use a better fit?

Day 57:   PURPLE ROBE

Every journey has a secret destination of which the traveler is unaware. Martin Buber, quoted in the Bangor, Maine, <u>Daily News</u>

The purple robe, an eye-catching eccentricity, has mesmerized botanists for years with its elegant "violet cups." This flower prefers a habitat of semi-shade where it bathes itself in nature's elements.

Humankind also lives under different shades. We conduct ourselves in inconsistent ways depending on who is watching what's going on. Surprisingly, at times we, too, are shocked by the actions of folks we believe we know very well.

There are countless reasons for fluctuations in behavior—depression, frustration, financial crisis, boredom or personal loss. When crossing the line from rational to irrational, know that life is full of choices.

Every pinch in which we find ourselves morphs with corridors. If we select the right ones, we raise the bar to greater possibilities. As the bar to greatness rises, the fence which traps us lowers. We can then pole-vault high above obstacles. Behind the scenes, a loving God is there to extend the length of our dowel or give us an extra boost.

DIANA LOUISE WEBB

Richard W. Siebels in <u>Friends Journal</u> (9/02) thrusts a meaningful gist into the conception of never having to go it alone. "There is an interconnectedness, a oneness, an interrelationship of all life. We are not separate, isolated beings, but are all part of the great mystery of creation."

Even in a sphere where evil and injustice are entrenched, God so loved the world that He sent His only begotten son[9] to teach and heal; to love and extend mercy.

Your goal: Find reconciliation with self.

<u>Day 58</u>:   FAIRY SLIPPER

Faith is the great energy. As long as you have faith, you're willing to try to take another chance. God wants you to amble toward the right spot on the horizon. The idea is that you're willing to get up and keep moving toward the light. Bill Corgan, songwriter

If you could meet the mate of your dreams and share the best time of your life, knowing that three months later, he or she would die, would you still have wanted to share the experience or would you have rather chosen to pass the opportunity by?

My friend, Kelli, was faced with such a dilemma. She met Steve the day after Thanksgiving in 1995. He was a charming, athletic college student studying engineering. Kelli spent the day at the mall—early Christmas shopping. Steve was picking up a tux for his brother's wedding. While leaving the rental boutique, his cummerbund slipped off the hanger onto the floor. My friend happened to be walking through the complex foyer at the exact same time. She picked up the sash and followed Steve in an effort to return the item. It was not until they both reached the parking lot that Kelli flagged him down.

Waving, she yelled, "Hey, you dropped something."

Just then, Steve turned toward her. His dimples deepened as a lively expression reeled its way across his face. Speechless, Kelli could only stare in bewilderment. It was love at first sight.

The winsome fellow then asked, "Uh, I'm going to a wedding tonight—it's actually my brother who is getting married. I am the

---
[9] John 3:16

THE BUTTERFLY COMETH

Best Man. This is going to sound really crazy, but do you want to go with me?"

All Kelli could squeeze out was a soft, "Yeah, sure."

When I first heard the story, I could hardly believe it because something like that only happens in the movies.

Kelli, an elementary school teacher, grew up in the Rocky Mountains. She never dated much as she engrossed herself in studies; thus, never had time for a serious relationship.

That night, sky rockets and Roman candles ignited into the wee hours of the morning. Dolled up in a bamboo twill linen evening frock, Kelli kicked off her slingbacks and the couple danced till sunrise.

"Steve," she whispered, "I feel like I have known you all my life. I don't want tonight to end."

The night eventually did come to an end. On the drive home, the sun peeked over the skyline.

"I want to take you somewhere special, but let's get a little sleep first," Steve stated. "I'll pick you up at about 12:30."

Beaming, Kelli skipped into her apartment. She couldn't sleep. She couldn't eat. She couldn't even sit. Rather than relaxing for a few hours until lunch, my smitten friend jumped into the shower and then whipped up a picnic basket packed with delicious fried chicken and homemade potato salad.

Kelli revealed her thoughts to me about Steve in terms of a phrase set forth by children's literature author, Sandol Stoddard Warburg: "If you and I had some drums and some horns and some horses; if we had some hats and some flags and some fire engines, we could be a whole parade!"

At 12:30, Steve arrived greeting his maiden with the same deep-dimpled grin as in the parking lot the day before. He drove her to a lovely wooded forest expressing excitement and pleasant surprise for his newfound love's kindness in preparing a meal. Hand-in-hand, the two walked through the luscious emerald grove. Steve reached down and picked up a precious fairy slipper, presenting it to his princess. Kelli gazed at the resilient flower and then into Steve's captivating brown eyes.

"You are not the man of my dreams because my dreams are not this wonderful."

Diana Louise Webb

Taking Kelli's hand, Steve replied, "You're right. I am not the man of your dreams. Before this goes any further, I must tell you something." Hesitating for a moment, he slowly continued, "I have been diagnosed with lymphoblastic leukemia. It's a battle I have fought for almost a year and a suitable bone marrow match cannot be found. At best, the doctors say I have three months to live."

Kelli fell to her knees. Maintaining it was better to have not loved at all than to have loved and lost, Kelli ended the friendship with Steve. She did not have the gumption to step out in faith.

Ten years later and still single, my friend shared her misgivings.

"I kept the fairy slipper, dried in my Bible. It's a reminder that when someone puts a boot in our path and we stick our foot into it, lace it up, and snap on the buckle, we have to wear it. Some people wait their whole life to find what I had. I willingly lost it in two days. Sometimes, a certain song will play on the radio, or I will sense the essence of his cologne and reminisce ... I guess those memories will always be with me."

On earth, we become so entwined in the "me, me, me" of our existence that we forget to reach around our egotism, which causes us to lose hope. Then our pace is feverishly accelerated in an effort to not miss a thing, but we miss everything that really matters. One day becomes just like the next—walking zombies who are so disgruntled by what we are facing—that we are not thankful for what lies before us. We bypass prosperity. In that mode, life is an unfulfilling wreck. We refuse to believe in the unknown or wait to see how things pan out. We work on our time, not God's time.

Norman Vincent Peale, in <u>The Power of Positive Thinking</u>, urges us to live at God's rate so we may behold peace and not miss our blessing. In essence, God says, "Go ahead if you must with this foolish pace and when you are worn out, I will offer my healing. But I can make your life so rich if you slow down now and live and move and have your being in me."

Kelli could have enjoyed a fabulous lifetime with Steve—regardless of the number of days. Companions are the medicine of life. When you meet that one special person who becomes your parade, embrace his or her heart. Hold it delicately and close to your heart. It is deserving of nurturing. As a pair, be the duke and duchess.

THE BUTTERFLY COMETH

Say, "I love you" often. Be a best friend, a confidant and an advocate.

All of us are destined to have the finest regardless of time. We make bold moves and some of them work; some of them don't. But we shouldn't worry about it. Leave the worrying to God. That's His job. Once we step into the next world, we will finally come to know the answer to the question, "Why was I so concerned about those other things?"

Query: Are you still wedged?

Day 59:   CHAMOMILE

Goodness is the only investment that never fails. Henry David Thoreau

Chamomile, a potent weed used in medicines or tea to cure ills, has been proven as an effective aid in the bailiwick of natural remedies.

In the same way we cleanse our bodies from sickness, we need to distil ourselves from sin. When contaminated, we consume our own motives and attempt to give orders to the one above about how life should progress for us.

As part of creation, we are within God's handiwork. When we become detached from the blanket of life, the hook breaks off our crochet needle and the yarn of a prolific future unravels. But when the heart's purpose is fixed on a devotion of principled living, God tailors a palatial afghan for us which answers love's call.

Swaddled in His adoring arms, we realize the kinetic spread of love deices the multitude of hearts that behold God's linens. Only with cleansing preparation can we fully accept the inheritance.

Cognition of the hour: Are you answering God's call?

Day 60:   COCA

That "what should be" never did exist, but people keep trying to live up to it. There is no "what should be," there is only what is. Lenny Bruce

Diana Louise Webb

The Putumayo rain forest of Colombia is a rural farming district centrally located in South America. A poverty-stricken people, the Pueblos sustain themselves by growing crops such as corn, rice and Heart of Palm. The coca plants grow wild and are chewed as a daily pick-me-up, much like caffeine perks us up in colas, tea and coffee.

As part of the War on Drugs, the American government is trying to exterminate coca, even though it cannot be used as black market cocaine without added chemicals imported from the U.S. The peaceful natives do not harbor the coca for illegal sales. It is only part of their culture, as natural as baseball and apple pie are to Americans. The grave concern is that U.S. aerial fumigation efforts raze not only the coca plants, but also ruin huge crop yields as a collateral effect.

My friend, Mary Barr, an author and motivational speaker, toured the Putumayo region to grasp a better understanding of "Plan Colombia." This plan is the U.S. sponsored program which gave farmers a one-time payment of $2,000 in livestock or seed for corn, rice or Heart of Palm. Mary shared with me that the project incorporated a contract for farmers to burn off any coca and to be placed on a list for fumigation. Even if one farmer in the locale agreed, all were forced to agree or no payment would be rendered.

Native, Don Ishmael, his wife, and cousin, led Mary to three farms.

Mary relayed, "In walking for miles we saw no coca, yet they all had been fumigated, the last time only two days before. At one patch of Heart of Palm, the senora stopped me and started to cry. I guess she was around sixty years old, and she had spent days in the blasting heat of the region to plant these crops. The crops were totally devastated. She told me it was the third time she planted and had her crops fumigated. Then she said something that made me grab an interpreter thinking my Spanish was faulty. She repeated that these were Plan Colombia crops. The very crops we had paid her and given her seed and instruction to plant! And we had fumigated them not once, but three times. Of all the things I learned, this tiny crying woman moved me the most."

The U.S. embassy in Colombia revealed to Mary that over 8,000 complaints had been filed regarding foiled extermination attempts. Of these, only two had been paid out for a total of $6,000.

THE BUTTERFLY COMETH

With water sources contaminated, animals afflicted with diseases, toxic chemicals sickening the local population and no money or harvests in sight, it is not the drug dealers who suffer.

Claiming to solve a problem and actually solving one can be a score that may only be bridged by an abutment not of man's government. This arc is kindred correspondence—infinite and unlimited. Found solitarily in our Creator, it is the power of one—not two, three or any number in the flesh.

Your faith summons into being that which you cogitate. Your world then becomes a genesis of your reflections. Those same thoughts are a ring in the unification of humankind to solve international problems. All of the rings across sea and land band together—a great melting pot blended by the blood of universal kinship.

Be an active part of the transitional effort!

Day 61:   WOOLLY YARROW

Man's main task in life is to give birth to himself to become what he potentially is. The most important product of his effort is his own personality. Erich Fromm

Fernlike and sprouting pocket-sized canary buds, the hardy woolly yarrow creates pixie charm. It is a popular plant—accommodating every botanical guru, even the one who lacks a green thumb. The woolly yarrow can withstand drought, the salty air and poor soil conditions, which make it desirable as a runner or edging for a greensward.

As human beings, we can also withstand drought in our lives if we vest our seed in God instead of planting it in the hands of man. Nothing is too raw to be brought before God. He is the one who can add nutrients to our ground, open the Heavens for a swish of refreshing rainwater and till our compacted dirt. He is the "Miracle-Gro" of the spiritual realm—an essence which transcends into our current reality to remind us the Gold Cup is yet to come.

The misfortune is that we sift out our "Miracle-Gro" because we keep utilizing the human method as opposed to God's method. Thus, we measure with our minds and rationalize out the inconceivable resolutions.

As you venture through the Mojave to spot fertile ground, signal your Intrepid Explorer within. He will lead you to an abundant ebullient watering hole where you can fill your canteen to reach a horticultural extravaganza. If the trail gets cold, remain expectantly hopeful. At high noon, a Humvee will be your chariot out of the sands. Taking your place on the comfy passenger bucket seat, you will ride into the bountiful foliage of a glamorous chaparral.

Day 62:   FOUR-LEAF CLOVER

The ability to have or to find information when you need it and then take action is what gets things done in life. Julio Melara

When we are attentive to a matter, we prosper. God continually divulges new thoroughfares to us. Some refer to these blessings as luck, brought about by icons such as four-leaf clovers. Although infrequent and uncommon to find, the four-leaf clover is a symbol of good fortune.

On a more powerful stratum, Lady Luck only arrives on the scene if God makes it happen. And God will do that. He just asks that we meet him halfway.

This networking may be seen with clarity in a story told by a priest. There was a Christian man—a passionate laborer for Christ—who prayed to win the lottery. He was a man with a mission of serving God, citing, "Lord, the lottery is $15,000,000. I could do so much for you if I won."

That week, no one won and the enormous jackpot rolled over.

Then worth $125,000,000, the man appealed, "God, this is tremendous. A bigger pot will feed and clothe more homeless."

The next week came and once more, the man did not win. The jackpot increased to a whopping $350,000,000.

Again, the man prayed that he would be the one.

"Abba Father, I know you know I have worthy plans for the money and I am here to tend to your flock. I am ready. The jackpot has surpassed what I imagined. Let this week be the time."

THE BUTTERFLY COMETH

The following day, a winner was announced—the sole recipient of the $350,000,000. But it was not the man hoping to save the world. Befuddled, he gazed at Heaven, claiming, "Almighty Creator, my life is devoted to you. I had high hopes for using the winnings to buy blankets for the poor, to purchase medicine for the sick and to feed the hungry. I wanted to give shelter to the destitute and pay for glasses for the needy and essentials for the deprived. I made arrangements for a water purification system in the inner city and to build a baseball diamond in the projects. I don't understand why you didn't want me to win ...".

A voice thundered overhead, "My son, I wanted you to win. But to hit the jackpot, you have to meet me halfway. You have to at least buy a ticket!"

It is God, not serendipity, who is our wheel of fortune. Our lot is not regulated by lucky charms. Shaped by the Lord, His navigation directs us. However, we must meet him halfway.

When you chip in, life spins a partnership wherein two halves make a whole. In the center is a spiral consisting of God the Father, Christ His Son and the Holy Spirit—three in one. From this Holy Trinity begins your most important work: realizing your relationship with God is the closest possible union you will ever know.

This week: Buy a ticket!

Day 63:   CARNATION

Who knows what women can be when they are finally free to become themselves? Who knows what women's intelligence will contribute when it can be nourished without denying love? Betty Friedan

On the road to Calvary, Jesus' mother walked with her son. A woman of strength, faith and devotion, Mary believed Jesus to be more than her beloved son. She knew Him as the Messiah. Only through this revelation could Mary endure. Her example lives with us.

Mothers are very special. It all begins with the creation of woman. The glorious miracle of why God created woman lies in the inner radiance for which a woman stands. He chose to create her from the rib of man[10] so she would not be above him or below him, but always at his side. God chose His beloved creation on the Sixth Day—the day before he adorned rest. Her angelic splendor and delicate intricacies reflect God's own image.

Instilled in woman is a nurturing ability and a protective maternal instinct. Just as the rib guards and protects, so, too, does a woman shield her child from harm. She provides direction and fosters emotional support. A woman embraces intuition—a "Sixth Sense" from being created on the "Sixth Day."

A woman presents an incandescent glow which illuminates those with whom she comes into contact. She has a knack for fixing almost anything with a Band-Aid and a smile. Her heart beams with affection and gentleness. It brims with love.

In honor of motherhood, in the early 1900s, a woman from Grafton, West Virginia, named Anna Jarvis, started a campaign for a national day of recognition. To celebrate a mother's love, she chose the second Sunday in May and incorporated the custom of wearing a carnation as part of the jubilee.

On May 9, 1914, President Woodrow Wilson recommended the observance as an annual commemoration calling the day of tribute "Mother's Day." It was officially proclaimed the next year.

The mother's love I hold near and dear is that of my own mother. She is my hero. But each one of us has parental inclinations irrespective of whether we are biological mothers or not. Thus, we, too, can be a celebrated impetus of motherhood. Our love is immeasurable as professed by Zelda Fitzgerald's saying, "Nobody has ever measured, not even poets, how much the heart can hold."

As you venture out and answer the invitation to be a "Mother to All," share your love with blessings of amity. Braid in the maternal secrets you learned from your own mother or female superstar. Then Charleston your way to celebrating amazing motherhood by stepping to Fred Astaire's debonair dance philosophy: "Do it big! Do it right! Do it with style!"

---

[10] Genesis 2:22

THE BUTTERFLY COMETH

Day 64:   MORNING GLORY

Seek refuge in inner silence, free your thoughts from the external world and you will feel the rays of God's goodness and love pouring over you and the universe. Persian Wisdom

As the misty dew fades into the grassland at the break of a crisp, cool dawn, the morning glory opens its rich blossoms to greet a lovely morn.

We, too, have all had a day when we needed to let the dew soften us up. There will be many days to come when we should soak before rising, so we can sprout a little easier and have a blissful morning. Too often, we rush about and do not take the time to relax in silence to gather our thoughts, prepare for the day and acknowledge our Gardener above.

In silence, we gain a distinguished ideation of our relationship to God's friendly universe. The sweet spiritual communion gives renewed color to our activities. Reaffirming our promise, we turn our concerns over to God. Hence, we never lose the love for any tidbit which whorls through us—whether it is a disquieted restlessness or a striking rainbow.

From <u>The Brothers Karamazov</u> by Fedor Dostoevsky, "If you love each separate fragment, you will understand the mystery of the whole resting in God. When you perceive this, your understanding of this mystery will grow from day to day until you come to love the whole world with a love that includes everything, excluding nothing."

Lord, color my world with love!

Day 65:   CLARET-CUP CACTUS

Sweat is the cologne of accomplishment. Heywood Hale Brown quoted in <u>Real Simple</u>

Simple and serene, the claret-cup cactus finds its niche in the most humble of abodes. Its needs are few; its offerings, many. A dignified model of survival, the cactus abides through blistering temperatures with astonishing poise and temperance.

Diana Louise Webb

We, as humans, are a lot like the cactus. We are much stronger than for what we give ourselves credit. Believing we are weak, our affirmations are not as confident as they could be. When we cannot have what we want immediately, we falter; we give up. We succumb to misery. But most people do not care whether we are miserable or happy so we might as well free ourselves from the suffering.

An amazing story about winning and courage in the face of disaster is the phenomenal self-rescue of rock climber Aron Ralston.[11] An eager adventurer, Aron set out on Saturday, April 23, 2003, to go hiking on a jaunt down Blue John Canyon on the outskirts of Canyonlands National Park in Utah. At age twenty-seven, Aron proved to be an experienced outdoorsman—skilled at his love for canyoneering.

Well into the remote canyon, Aron crossed paths with a boulder wedged in a narrow cleft. As he maneuvered over the rock, it shifted compressing his right arm against the sidewall. Aron was literally immobilized and corralled with no relief in sight. He did not tell anyone where he was going that day nor could he be seen in the shadows of Blue John Canyon.

Days passed. Aron had run out of water and food, and the chilling thirty-degree evening temperatures numbed his t-shirt clad body.

By the following Thursday, Aron faced the grim reality of either rescuing himself or dying in Blue John Canyon. Braving the unthinkable, he prepared to sever his right limb. Realizing he could not amputate his arm with a pocketknife, the only tool he had with him, Aron broke his radius and ulna and then cut the connective tissue.

This exhausted, yet determined young man, rappelled seventy feet and hiked five miles where he chanced upon a couple with a child also on an outing. Help was called and a helicopter arrived to transport Aron to the hospital. He survived.

With the use of an artificial limb, resoluteness and a 'never-give-up' attitude, Aron continues to rock climb and enjoy all the activities he engaged in prior to his injury.

---

[11] Ralston, Aron. <u>Between a Rock and a Hard Place</u>. Aron Ralston, 2004. By permission.

THE BUTTERFLY COMETH

In the midst of the terrible incident, Aron's will to live intensified via a premonition that drifted into his mind while stuck at Blue John. He pictured a little boy running into the loving embrace of a one-armed man. Aron concluded he was the man, and the tiny tot—the son he would father one day.

God gives us strength and hoists us up through our dreams, the practice of prayer and confident affirmations. Steve Maynard, in a selection entitled <u>Affirming Acceptance</u>, exalts our confidence in the Lord with his interpretation of the best way to "go forward" in situations where the only way to "move forward" is to see through the eyes of God. Steve writes, "Praying for 'acceptance' shifts our focus from a confrontation with the 'facts' to a connection with them. As we do this, we begin coming to peace with situations—opening ourselves to truly seeing God in the circumstances that surround us. We open ourselves to see and experience divine order and divine wisdom at work in our lives."

Candidly receive Aron's courage and self-assurance. Capture the breath of prayer. Affirm the positive. Now look in the mirror and rejoice because just as the cactus is an integral part of nature, you, too, are an integral part of God.

<u>Day 66</u>:   FORGET-ME-NOT

All I can say is this: last one out, please turn on the lights. Rod Norland, <u>Newsweek</u>

The vivacious, resplendent bounty of the forget-me-not proffers the assumption that this flower will be anything but forgotten. The message reminds me of my friend, Julie.

A beautiful and artistic woman, Julie, is the epitome of living in simple abundance. Her craftsmanship enables her to create functional components and decorative trinkets out of almost nothing. Converting used toilet tissue rolls into attractive Santa dolls with the help of a few cotton balls and red construction paper, Julie's talent and influence far exceed paper creations. She emulates humanity's quest for a happy life through her service of love which lasts a lifetime.

Julie explained to me one day, "Diana, wherever you go, people are the same. Faces change. Names change. The people remain the same. In delving into freshness, it is the negativity we need to leave behind. We may then experience the true grit of a joyful spirit and love defined outside of this world."

The family of man is hungry by instinct. We strive for love; however, most of us only engineer the love our world profiles: I love you because …

This love will not flow freely. Why? Because we have clogged the pipe. We do not know the story so we don't know how to free up the blockage. The oddity is that this is not a story to be broadcasted on a platform. No, this story's platform is our everyday life. It is living the message of how to eddy the spigot. It is bringing others to feel God through how we live our faith by example.

Jesus lived a rich life because of His relationship with the presence of the Father. You, too, can live "life" as a consciousness of God—a love that knocks the world off its axis.

You are love, life and wisdom. Start knocking!

Day 67:   MILKWEEDS

Forgiveness: the fragrance the violet sheds on the heel that has crushed it. Mark Twain

Pesky and irritating, milkweeds unexpectedly spring up corrupting the most fair and lovely of flowerbeds. Undiscriminating, they bogart their way into Heaven's masterpieces staining what are otherwise iridescent doting fields of the perfumes of spring.

But the flowers are forgiving. They make room and share the sunlight with the uninvited guests. What a pity that humans are not so amiable. When we are offended, we tend to harbor an undercover grudge by purporting to forgive, but we cannot forget. By not forgetting, is it genuinely forgiving?

Obviously in life, it sounds good to tell someone, "Ah, just forget it," but in all reality, we cannot forget something that happened. If it happened, it happened, and we will remember it happened. But what we can do is forgive because we want forgiveness for the punches we lob.

THE BUTTERFLY COMETH

When we fail to extend others the same forgiveness that Jesus gave to us when He was betrayed, nailed to a cross, ridiculed and denied, we cordon off prospects to have the splotches of our indiscretions removed. Luke 6:37 tells us, "Forgive and you will be forgiven." If we don't, we permanently seal our smudges. We give way to a stain to which even Clorox throws up its hands.

By forgiving, we are not handing out a license for others to keep hurting us. We are just exhaling past pain, resentment and bitterness. We are also exhaling our desire for spiteful retaliation and giving up our right to hold a grudge. Giving our hearts back their elasticity, we pass on the hemlock cocktail which is slowly killing us.

Forgive and you will always find forgiveness galloping over the horizon—patiently and lovingly waiting just for you.

Day 68:   ENGLISH IVY

There is a period of life where we swallow a knowledge of ourselves and it becomes either good or sour inside. Pearl Bailey

Impressively built on Camelback Mountain, surrounded by thirty-foot towering walls, the renowned Arizona landmark, "the castle," is a curiosity for all.

Featuring a sixteen-foot waterfall and many ornate amenities, this historical estate recently hit the sales market sporting a price tag of $10,000,000. Although the terrain encircling the manor flaunts a sandy dune, English ivy spotlights the front stone patio. Its waxy luster compliments as a magnificent addition to an already breathtaking structure.

Vibrant and spry, the ivy parades a pert evergreen carpet amidst the cobblestone. Even in the roughest of landscapes, the ivy thrives.

Let's imagine ourselves as ivy plants. What do we do when we are struggling in the thick of experiences which are not so fragrant? We are inclined to let go of what we have going for us and allow the stench to overtake. Before we know it, we are "caught up"— swimming in quicksand and rapidly sinking. Inundated with muck, we are squelched. Our glass has tipped over.

This year, fill your glass!

"It is all within yourself, in your way of thinking," remarks Marcus Aurelius. To the degree that the future is concerned, you are not credited on the decision of others. You are set apart by how you lead. Ultimately, the common threads of your tenacity and your reason for being align flush left. As your whole life then lies ahead of you, you will spy the clues even among the patches of darkness. When you do, land your best shot!

Day 69:   BLEEDING HEART

You must not lose faith in humanity. Humanity is an ocean; if a few drops of the ocean are dirty, the ocean does not become dirty. Mahatma Gandhi

Named for its heart-shaped blossoms that arch in rows on a vine, the bleeding heart symbolically limns a crushed or forlorn dream—the very bereavement met by all mortals. It is during defeating stretches when we could use revitalizing comfort the most. In inconsolable and dejected moments, we are not peerless. Not only have others borne similar situations, Jesus Himself, writhed in pain, more than we ever will bear.

Our woes pale in comparison. Therefore, whatever disheartening event we are up against, God's love is much, much greater. In searching for solace, our hearts once again become pliable through the holy tears shed. Healing may not be instantaneous. Just as a toddler takes baby steps before he can walk, we may be steered to various places or through steps or stages before we become adept in the comprehensive itinerary.

Whether things are falling in place or out of place, God is with us. Be with God and reciprocate. Reach for a Bible instead of a cell phone or laptop in both times of sorrow and joy. Delight in the consolation of scripture. If your heart must bleed, be pleased in the security that you are not sequestered alone. The Bible is only a book away.

THE BUTTERFLY COMETH

Day 70:   CREEPING BUTTERCUP

Conscience is the perfect interpreter of life. Karl Barth

Indigenous to the hottest continents, the creeping buttercup "creeps" up yearly to a height of twelve inches. In the wild or in backyard gardens, its presence is not requested although it is a quite pleasing enhancement to the environment.

How many times do we assume the role of the creeping buttercup and thrust ourselves into situations that do not involve us: a friend's dispute, a couple's relationship or our own extended family's issues? Regardless, we feel it necessary to throw in our two cents to yield "flowery" results that meet our satisfaction. Overcasting the scuff, we saturate so heavily in the affairs of others that families split up and wedges are driven between friends.

Sometimes, no matter how ambrosial our intentions, making it our business to be in someone else's business can break the trust and confidence built by mates and companions and kinfolk. The paradox is that we intervene under the auspices of improving the plight when, in reality, we seek to please our own basic desire for control. We surrogate as a gauze pad—absorbing the emotions of other people.

If a pickle wells up that affects an individual in your private circle, think before interjecting yourself into the mix. If the words you find imperative to orate or the deeds you contemplate are nothing more than rumormongering or scandalizing, obviously the parties concerned will not appreciate the meddling.

A distinction may be drawn between interfering and interceding. Earmark the distinction and recognize stepping in when a comrade has stepped out and warrants reeling in as the right thing to do. You are forever called into stewardship, but never summoned to comport as a busybody.

In good graces, stick to your own knitting.

Day 71:   GOLDEN ROD

The best part of a good man stays forever, for love is immortal and makes all things immortal. But hate dies every minute. William Saroyan, USA Today

Diana Louise Webb

In the genius of approximately 100 species of woody-based perennials, the golden rod is an attractive hybrid comprised of clusters of saffron-colored flowers. With water and lots of sunshine, the golden rod cavalcades as a honey lamp of Heaven.

Our life on earth can also be as golden as we want it to be. Not withstanding, going overboard with self-flattery and bragging only sharpen the edge of burning spasms. The braggart personality type reckons his or her value outside of self since there is no love stemming from within. Low or no self-esteem stymies any naturalness impeding a "what you see is what you get" image. Hollow sounds modulate from a shell striated with a gallery of credentials not worth their weight in air. Exaggerated credentials or any credentials boasted are false identities as the actual and valid identity rests upon who we are in Christ.

Obsessions with self need to be moved to the side before God can move within us. Charles Solomon makes the fundamental assertion in his book, <u>Handbook to Happiness,</u> that when self is in control, "we use our own will and mind to run our lives, instead of only using them in the doing role. In other words, we are doing in order to be rather than being in order to do. As a result, we are less effective in living. If God is running our lives, then our mind, emotions, and will are free to serve his purposes unhampered by the additional duties of trying to decide how we should live our lives."

Make this a golden moment to be like the golden rod. Let amber emissions stream across your heart with the same royalty as that of Mother Earth in the promise of the rainbow after an invigorating spring shower. The rainbow makes room for all its lively colors to sashay in unison. Make room in your life for God to do the same. The opportunity is golden—truly golden.

<u>Day 72</u>:   BABIES'-BREATH

Some rise by sin and some by virtue fall. William Shakespeare, <u>Measure for Measure</u>

Delicate and adored, when babies'-breath bedecks an arrangement, it brings the posies to life with the same love as seen in a mother's eyes after giving birth to a newborn. God bestowed upon us the beloved gift of procreation. What God has given, man does not have the right to take away or manipulate.

Too often, man cannot resist the temptation to play God. Science has trespassed onto God's sacred grounds by probing the provinces of controversial experimentation, including cloning and embryonic stem-cell research. Advocates of suspect causes claim that those who disfavor the projects simply fail to comprehend the enlightenment behind them. This is not true.

Opponents of embryonic stem-cell research do not resist technological headway. These supporters just will not welcome raping human dignity as part of civilization's advancement. In fact, they adamantly support the use of the millions of stem cells that are destroyed daily from umbilical cords after birth. Those cells are workable prospects which do not violate God's law.

The world is a laboratory. Methodical research, which does not supercede God, never conflicts with faith because scientific breakthroughs derived from man and miracles derived from faith are given by the same God. God never denies Himself.

Human life, by natural right, should be safeguarded at the most vulnerable stages. Those in power have a responsibility not to strong-arm anyone for the upper hand. Their allegiance is to the people, not their respective parties. When they don't revere that charge, protections afforded mummify. The comparable happens when we, as citizens, fail to respect and be faithful to our own convictions. By compromising our ethical standards, they eventually turn to stone.

Par with the duty of the government to maintain the utmost in trustworthiness and honesty and to avoid overreaching, we must meet with the equivalent and proceed with integrity.

Standing behind a fact-finding mission to advance our body of knowledge is a valuable benefit. When chartered without anesthetizing our inherent good, a discovery quest is a wonderful way to gain strides to make the world a better place. However, the wisdom of Albrecht Moritz goes without reproach. His philosophical paradigm: "Science that ignores ethics is bad science, no matter what 'progress' it makes."

Question for the day: Have you eaten from the insane root?

Diana Louise Webb

Day 73:   HOLLYHOCK

Some days you tame the tiger. And some days the tiger has you for lunch. Ballplayer Tug McGraw

First brought to the West in the sixteenth century from China, the hollyhock quickly won favor by its long blooming season, a span from the middle of the summer to the early fall.

Genuineness should enjoy a similar course—a long, honest serving of being. Artificiality can be spotted right away and is most insulting when dealing with apologies. Saying "I'm sorry" and meaning it are worlds apart.

It is our own pride, fear, shame and conceit that hold us captive in making a frank apology. Confessing would mean we have disobeyed God. But God is merciful. If we confess our sins, He will cleanse us from everything we have done wrong (1 John 1:9).

Admitting we are wrong is difficult, but if we can get over the arrogance hurdle, we are half there. This conversion's implications are the work of a lifetime. When we forge a sham, we ignore God altogether. This involuntary servitude is submission to the master of bondage: the enemy being self.

God breaks the chains of slavery. Do you dare to choose such freedom?

Day 74:   VENUS'S-FLYTRAP

It don't mean a thing if it ain't got that swing. Duke Ellington

Different, yet sophisticated, Venus's-flytrap is most unusual. Insectivorous, it devours meat in claw-like traps to sustain itself in comparison to the traditional soil and water combo absorbed by fellow genres.

In life, just because someone is different does not denote inferiority. Our planet resembles a giant shopping center—something for everyone. Any less would dilute the fascination and appeal of the individual contribution.

From construction workers to pharmacists, from astronauts to filing clerks, from waitresses to professors, each person bears a potter's wheel in sculpting creation's cooling fires. In affable oneness, we work together to fulfill the purpose of God's grand fête. The velocity sparks a natural intonation.

Part of being a member of a community is honoring the importance of the other members. Communities grow. The affiliates' differences add to healthy diversity. They challenge the mind and provide stimulation to void any flatness. In the acts that we do, know that a community is molded by doing what we, as individuals, can do with what we have right where we are.

In the terrarium of life, what is your unique contribution?

Day 75:   CATTAIL

If you find two four-leaf clovers, you give me one. If I find four, I give you two. If we only find three, we keep on looking. Sandol Stoddard Warburg

Pretend you are on the bank of a river. You spot a small weathered bottle stuffed with a cork floating amongst the cattails. As you reach in between the dense, brown thicket, and down into the murky medley of grasses and little critters, you retrieve the glass vessel. Leaves concealed the decanter for over a decade.

You pop the cork only to find a message written on thin parchment paper stuck inside. The communiqué reads, "I'll always remember every single tear you shed for me. Drop your leaves, dear Helen. Drop your leaves."

You lay back on the meadow perplexed as to the significance of the note. *Hmmm… What does it mean?*

Max Lucado spoke about tears, "It's not just tears that are the issue, it's what they represent. They represent the heart, the spirit and the soul of a person. To put a lock and key on your emotions is to bury part of your Christlikeness."

Could this be part of the translation? Hmmm…

To two people out there somewhere the meaning is clear. Words disclose very intense and important points. When pen is put to paper, the theme amplifies. Written correspondence is an excellent way to express self and to attain a welding of being with another person.

Diana Louise Webb

When you tender written words, how does it feel? Is there a bond between you and the receiver that only the two of you understand?

Right now is the A-1 time to load your pocket protector with fountain pens and pencils. Pack in stationery accompanied with a barrage of inventiveness and globetrot on an expedition from your heart to your hands. As the creativity rolls in, roll out a true Shakespeare via a spectral plume. Spread colorful wishes, affectionate memories, heartfelt declarations and impassioned feelings.

Tonight, write.

Day 76:   TUBEROUS BEGONIA

A man who moved a mountain was the one who began carrying away small stones. Chinese Proverb

Displayed in public conservatories for their presentation of big lavish floral bursts, begonias serve as dynamic conversation pieces. Flaring in all colors except blue, these beauties are native to South America.

What the begonia lacks in an elongated, sparse stem, it compensates in opulent florets, sometimes so replete the stem is weighed down necessitating staking the plant.

Squaring with the begonia, we can be weighed down, too. But the weight which pulls us south may countervail as might to help us excel in other areas.

An inspirational begonia in my life was my friend, Andrea, a charismatic, green-eyed Irish girl. Andrea lived life in a wheelchair. At age eight, while swimming at a lake during a family reunion, she dove off a pier into what was believed to be deep water. It wasn't. Sand obscured the bottom of a shallow three-foot basin. Andrea broke her neck and severed her spinal cord, rendering her a quadriplegic. She has since died, but her memory lives on.

Despite the consequences, Andrea found moving self-assurance in the story of Karen Casper, a paraplegic sports champion. Karen suffered a rare form of cancer destroying the nerve cells in her legs as a baby. She never walked, but refused to accept defeat—winning trophies, ribbons and medals for international wheelchair games.

THE BUTTERFLY COMETH

Like Karen, Andrea patterned a motto that "you've been given these cards, so you play them." She espoused the concept that if life shortchanges you in one area, a full hand in another will reimburse you. In both cases, you need to be grateful.

There are many things in life which are uncertain, but remain confident in God's intelligence and wisdom. When we are faithful, when we think we have reached Tap City, we discover Nirvana.

Andrea accepted her challenge with an open mind and an expectation of new opportunities. Unexpected blessings far-exceeding the imaginable happened. She lived a full life.

With faith, a hardy spirit accomplishes mountainous tasks. Coax forth your hardy derring-do as you commit to the work which God has prepared. This is your commission. Oblige. Welcome the challenge. Perform!

Day 77:   DANDELION

Sacred Friend, be with us this day. Within us to purify us; Above us to draw us up; Beneath us to sustain us; Before us to lead us; Behind us to restrain us; Around us to protect us. St. Patrick

Gazing across my neighbor's pasture late one evening, I noticed that what shone as a charming field of dandelions during the day, tucked itself into a still coverlet of resting decoratives at night.

Likening to the dandelion, on swarthy days, we may also close off. It is in the process of opening back up wherein the struggle chronically deadlocks. This bubble we form around ourselves may be a result of criticism or constant rebuking from others.

It is no secret that each one of us enjoys giving criticism. Responsible living dictates employing constructive techniques when conveying a comment. Approaching a situation with tact, diplomacy, good manners and sensitivity will increase a party's receptiveness.

That being said, we are privileged to evaluate an opinion for exactly what it is: an opinion. We may accept it, reject it or just let it marinate. We may share the impression or disregard it.

The concluding result is that an unbiased and non-judgmental exchange cultivates a sociable ambience. Thus, the locker in which we store our "off limits" box of non-negotiable thoughts drops its walls. Without walls, there is no need for doors; no need for locks. The multitude of knowledge that hovers around us sweetly percolates into the vast dimension of ourselves. If we still choose to be a sleeping ornamental, it will solely be a forty-wink snooze. Calling it a day by laying in a psychological coma molts away. Our brilliance, no longer siphoned off by our critics, proceeds with love on the Agape level.

As you catch the Agape wave, unreservedly coif your petals, straighten your stem and look around—the whole world is blooming.

Day 78:   PEACE LILY

Love is our shared truth. Peace is our eternal hope. The Museum of World Religions – Taiwan

The peace lily, scientifically known as Spathiphyllum, spurts long, oval leaves and pure sheaths designed to protect its main structure. Nicknamed "white flag," the peace lily lives up to its epithet, a symbol of surrender or yielding.

The world today needs to do a little yielding. Stubbornness lurks about inviting its uncle, self-centeredness, over for a row. On a worldwide scaffold, take a few minutes and resonate on the friction between nations, in particular, the United States and the Islamic world. Why do the people of the Middle East detest the United States?

A clear answer may be found in peace activist and Nobel Prize nominee, Kathy Kelly's book, Other Lands Have Dreams.[12] Kelly stands as a pillar in the Catholic Worker movement to encourage non-violent alternatives in making the world a more decent place to live. She advocates for universal humane treatment to combat the devastation wrought by war against civilians, especially children.

In response to the loathsome contempt buttressed against the U.S., Kelly concedes, "We take over and dominate over people's societies. We set up client states in their regions and rely on these

---

[12] Kelly, Kathy. Other Lands Have Dreams: From Baghdad to Pekin Prison. A K Press, 2005. By permission.

client states to house U.S. bases. We foster double standards, condemning invasion and occupation when it suits us (e.g., the Iraqi invasion of Kuwait) and yet undertaking or supporting murderous sanctions, invasions, and occupations, while claiming to support and enhance democratic states. Hideous and violent terrorist attacks will continue as long as we insist on taking other people's precious and irreplaceable resources for cut-rate prices. We should either begin paying fair prices, or find new ways to live in which we're not so dependent on these resources."

Granted, we would all sleep a little easier if terrorism were stamped out. When a tyrannical dictator falls from power, it is a peaceful relief. Moreover, there is no doubt weapons of mass destruction are threatening and need to be eliminated. The disagreement lies not in the objective; it roots in the deceit which peppers the legitimacy. Ulterior motives masquerade as worthy justice in hot pursuit of peace and security.

Unseating sinister demons merits cooperation, but not at the expense of destroying innocent people. Barbarous tactics of force do nothing other than wage war on ourselves, brutally shattering lives and hatching another callous generation trained to kill. The first casualty of war is peace; the next, truth.

Kathy Kelly posits, "Suppose we were to redirect just one billion dollars from our military budget to retrain doctors, nurses and water specialists who would be sent abroad, with no strings attached, to assist in neighboring countries? Wouldn't our security be enhanced if people in other lands viewed us as compassionate and generous people no longer addicted to war?"

Nonviolence, goodwill and humanitarianism begin with pragmatically thinking about what is at issue. It requires abandoning selfish motives and putting our "amour propre" on the back burner. With a peaceful approach, we may be intercontinental role models for all organizations, militia and otherwise.

Mentoring begins at home. Home is in the heart. And just like a dead heart has no life, the death of peace kills the soul.

Whether soldiers, children, or mothers or fathers ... whether Islamic or Jewish or Christian ... whether German, American, or Indian, the same true God created us. His message is one which ascends above nationality, uniforms and the "Shock and Awe" of war. He brings tidings of love and peace. He is the one who enables a tomorrow, one consisting of everything from missile makers becoming useful engineers to military med techs working in Third World hospitals. He can transform the hearts of hardened criminals into loving guidance counselors and redirect abortionists into the field of pediatrics.

For such an awesome tomorrow to materialize, we have to exhibit a willingness for love and peace to form our basis for decent living. We may outwardly reform corrupted ideals by inwardly warding off conflicts that choke the lifeblood from the capillaries of our peace lily.

Americans promenade our nation as the greatest country on earth. Obviously, we need to humbly adopt a little of that greatness and live simply so that others may simply live. Picketing the White House and singing It's a Small World doesn't get it anymore.

Ask yourself: For how long will you be content chewing the bitter leaf of self-serving exploitation?

Day 79:   INDIAN PAINTBRUSH

I could draw a circle on a piece of paper and my mother made me feel like Van Gogh. Damon Wayans

Holding its own as a colorful marshaling of captivation, the Indian paintbrush teaches us about beauty as it relates to the beholder. In other words, you either like it or you don't.

Because of variations in preference, two people may view the same scene, workmanship, or floral arrangement and form a divided fancy. Be that as it may, there is one who beholds all as a Raphael: He is God the Father, and His love is not divided. God's veiled attendance is present in all things—in trees and flowers, giving them life; in the planets and stars, giving them animation; in the denizens of the forest, giving them spirit; in the mountains and oceans, giving them vitality; and in you and me, giving us His graces.

As the world's Advocate, God's paintbrush colors all of creation. It is your decision to recognize His universe as a collection of Rousseau's greatest works of art or meaningless brush strokes.

THE BUTTERFLY COMETH

Indubitably, you may not request a smashed soup can to be first on your list for a mantelpiece, but by training your personal paintbrush, your radius of love will colorfully expand until it gives the whole world a Picasso.

Day 80:   BLUE HYACINTH

If a plant cannot live according to its nature, it dies; and so a human soul. Henry David Thoreau

While visiting friends in Nevada, I helped plant a serenity garden. At my suggestion, we sowed blue hyacinth. Doling out an aromatic scent, these flavorful clusters are well liked and appreciated.

The shoots were transplanted from a greenhouse. By lunchtime, the desert sand surrounding the home scrolled in an array of placid blue waves.

The next day, I woke up early to savor the odoriferous gems over a cup of hot cocoa. Taking a peek in between the blinds, I was overwhelmed with disappointment. My stately blue pièce de résistance morphed into droopy, wilted clumps.

I phoned a florist inquiring as to possible reasons for the sudden demise. The florist justified the fact that the parched ground was not the natural environment for the hyacinth. Outside its element, it could not survive.

This is analogous to our purpose as human beings. We are called to conform to a shape. When we pursue something outside of our God-given nature, we are like a circular block trying to fit into a triangular hole. It won't work.

"All that we are and all that we have comes from God," says Verna Dozier, author of <u>The Dream of God</u>. "We are part of God's dream for a good creation using our freedom to do God's will."

When we partake in the enchantment of life, fulfilling our purpose, the soul never dies. Inside the tent of knowing how to make a difference, we bask in the splendor of drawing out of ourselves and coming closer to what we are meant to be.

Diana Louise Webb

<u>Day 81</u>:　　MALTESE CROSS

My only purpose for being on the planet is to awaken to my God self!
Rev. Michael Beckwith, AGAPE Church of Religious Science

Bearing humble little bunches of scarlet crucifixes, the Maltese Cross is a spiritual sign that "this isn't it." We are headed for a final destination of eternal happiness; led by a road laden with earth's best. For if earthly joy, healing and supernatural wonders were to cease, it would mean God was destined to cease and that will never happen.

During our lifetime, we experience numerous trials. Gloom, pain and sickness are never God's plan. They only came about when man sinned and died spiritually. Regardless, our music box plays and we have a moral duty to keep it playing until "the Lord" calls us home.

In 2005, a highly controversial debate erupted involving right-to-die litigation. The estranged husband of Terri Schiavo, the woman who had been in a vegetative state for fifteen years, petitioned the court to have his wife's feeding tube removed. Against the wishes of Terri's parents and blood relatives, justice erred on the side of death and Schiavo's life support was terminated.

The ongoing battle commenced in 1990 when Schiavo, then twenty-six, collapsed in a hallway from a possible eating disorder. Deprived of oxygen, extensive brain damage caused Schiavo to lapse into a permanent vegetative condition. For the ensuing decade, loved ones, pitting against each other, fought for control of the fate of Terri Schiavo. But who are we to say who shall live and who shall die?

Creation is a miracle of love. Our lease on life is not of man's doing. Evidenced by the two words that begin the Lord's Prayer—"Our Father"—we can figure out who is in charge.

Hanging from a cross, God spoke the words, "It is finished." The end of His life on earth was a new beginning for mankind; a redemption from the curse of sin. What more could we ask?

This time of year, make an effort to thank God for your Maltese Cross—the receipt that your tab has been paid.

THE BUTTERFLY COMETH

Day 82:	JONQUIL

My soul can find no staircase to Heaven unless it be through Earth's beauty. Michelangelo

The meadow boasted a golden pond, a harvest of jonquils too hypnotic to even describe. Rich with life, rich with love, they enlivened my soul. But how do we "share" it?

Rod McIver in <u>Journal Notes</u> captures the magnificence of our journey in "Heron Dance" wherein he heralds that we "dive down, find the beauty, nurture it and offer it to the world ...". Furthering the concept, Wendy Crockett's <u>Sweetwater Wisdom</u> emphasizes we must not be judgmental; not be haled by ire, disdain and jadedness. We must keep active the intoxication of joy and passion for life. If we can no longer smell the fragrance, maybe we are the ones who need repotting.

Resurrecting our barren backyards, we release the perceptual frames which blacken the heart of morality's jewel, a gift never to be painted over. To receive, we have to appear true to self. Our truth, our incorruptibility, provide a restful satiety that asks nothing more. Within, we will come to know an innocence of heart, an infinite beauty to which all must return to unearth the completion of self.

In truth, go beyond and share yourself in the greater principle.

Day 83:	JACOB'S-LADDER

We don't have to be at the bottom. We were born to be at the top. The Thunder Brothers

Wouldn't it be great if we could climb our way up to Heaven? Unfortunately, we can't. But while we are here, we can be like Jacob's-ladder. We can climb to Christ-like greatness. Age, wisdom and experience, when sprinkled with God's love, make us more effective people—happier, healthier and purposeful.

Mirroring Jacob's-ladder as it sends up apple-green leaves crowned in sky-blue mini garnishes, we send forth a valuable education for generations to come as we grow. When advancing in years, we season—fine cheese flavored to perfection. We don't have to be the wrinkled up, cantankerous stereotype propagated by the media.

The handle of the door is on our end. We can open it to a hopeful, grand life or we can sit back in a rocking chair and pine with nostalgia of what could have been. Resisting living in youth's past is a hard mint to swallow if we can't accept the aging process.

As we get older, realization sets in that we won't ever be an Olympic athlete, naval aviator, or Miss Universe. However, we will always be a winner at heart and "receive" as part of God's gymnastic universe. That dream never fades away. Physical features, professions and labels eventually lose their color as the years trailblaze forward.

Keeping time with our perfected cheese, there comes a day when our cheese gets old. A foul smell penetrates our Gouda and suddenly everything stinks. Our cheese has slipped off the cracker.

What we obliviously then pitch into the disposal are our veteran qualities. We forget that if we pare off a few morsels of crusty dryness around the edges, we will again flare as a dandy Cheddar chef-d'oeuvre.

Today, let the child of renewal replenish your high hopes. Chuck your ladder and ride the escalator to the top floor. Life is too short to wait on energy to come strolling down the Boardwalk— cod liver oil in one hand, cane in the other.

Animals help us to connect to our spiritual intuition. So above, so below, they know we live in a field of unity. They are aware of the organic connection to the greater weave and tapestry of life. The animals have not forgotten the kingdom of love for it is their intuition and instinctual birthright to be a part of the greater whole.

Patty L. Luckenbach
<u>The Kingdom of Heart</u>

TRANSFORMATION
FROM "DOWN UNDER" ON SAFARI IN SYDNEY, AUSTRALIA

Change does not come without a struggle. As we "emerge," we must shake off our former habitat. We must rid ourselves of destructive surroundings. These include bad habits, paralyzed thinking and deadened feelings such as self-pity, guilt, anger and bitterness.

A day-by-day odyssey, Christel takes you "down under" on safari in Sydney, Australia. While she sheds her purlieu in fellowship with her friends of the animal kingdom, shed your faded layers. Peel back your onion coating. Breathe fresh quality into your intrinsic silk and flannel textile. Regain your indisputable force.

Explore your purpose!

Day 84:   Bee

Angels can unleash hurricanes of healing, release tidal waves of love, move whole mountains of hatred, melt icebergs of jealousy, and evaporate oceans of pain. Karen Goldman

As children trotting out to play, remember how we were constantly admonished, "Watch out for cars. Don't ride with strangers. Be home before dark." As we grew older, we still had to beware of the stings in life. However, with age came harsher lessons.

Just as the worker bee dies shortly after it thrusts one good sting into its target, it usually takes us only one good sting before we close off a part of ourselves. Suppressed without oxygen, trust eventually dies or the walls we build smash it. The stings that hurt the most are unfaithfulness, dishonesty and misplaced loyalty. When we are the "fall guy" to that type of pain, we shut down our vulnerability avenues. Feeling like we plummeted to the bottom of a cesspool, we must pause and dip our stings into a brook of healing water. The blood droplets clinging to our hearts are then washed away by the white incense of Heaven. Through the beating of sacred impulses, we are enlivened. Inundated with the deepest of senses, we once again open the turnstile of healthy vulnerability. If we later encounter stings, instead of conceding, we rub oil in our wounds. That brackish no longer has a place in either our hurts or our tears.

Your lens is focused. Your heart is home. Your vows are simple. Live so you may learn to love and love so you may learn to live.

Day 85:   Squirrel

Money and possessions are like diet soda—they satisfy momentarily, but they do not nourish. Kevin Anderson

Squirrels are interesting creatures. They make outside nests, preferably in pinewoods, or utilize holes made by woodpeckers to store their "stuff."

We live in a bureaucratic terrarium that also idolizes "stuff." In fact, most of us have difficulty making room to store all of our "stuff." We own homes with two- and three-car garages; yet, we cannot even park our cars in them because they are packed so full of "stuff." We rent storage buildings to store even more "stuff." We go to work each day to make more money to buy more "stuff" so we can attain more happiness. But does that really work? Does our "stuff" make us happy?

Reality dictates that no one says, "Bring me my Harley," on his or her deathbed. The chaplain of the church which I attend said he

THE BUTTERFLY COMETH

was just shy of performing 1,000 funerals. Never once during any of those services did he see a hearse followed by a U-Haul.

The undeniable truth is we cannot take our "stuff" with us. What we do take is the love we shared and the joyful memories of how we lived a Christ-filled life. As the soul departs the body, we take our presents of the heart with us. Nothing else matters any longer.

Day 86:   Barnacle

Champions don't become champions on the field—they are merely recognized there. Bob Costas

Resembling minuscule decapod crabs protected by six or eight calcareous plates, barnacles attach themselves to man-made structures and do the bare minimum to get through life.

Sounds familiar?

This scenario clearly pinpoints how we rob ourselves of life's adventure. If we skate through on the bare minimum to reach a destination, we deprive ourselves of the excitement of the safari. We live, but by not actualizing our potential, we subsist without reason. The future's drawing card lapses into a rut of stagnation since there are no peaks or valleys; no triumphs or defeats. We lose our zeal; we lose intimacy with self.

When our intimacy is lost, the relationship within us disintegrates into coal. The dire straits encroaching us multiply like barnacles cleaving to the decaying bottom of a dilapidated freighter. Before we know it, we are pulled under.

But with love and a little "gung-ho," we can reinstate the ardor. There is a better way. Whether by legs or in a Lamborghini, His grace is available to all of us. We just have to leave behind a life of putting faith in man. Man repeatedly disappoints. By living in the written inspiration of Christ, we are no longer weighed down by the barnacles. We are inebriated with the realization that the only power others have over us is that which is allowed from above. We have the ability to reclaim and regain.

The euphoria of life is the voyage. Don't let anyone heist that. More importantly, don't pirate it yourself. Go for the gusto!

Diana Louise Webb

Day 87:   DOVE

We all have the duty to work for peace. But in order to achieve peace, we should learn from Jesus to be meek and humble of heart. Matthew 11:29

The international symbol of peace, the dove, issues a taproot of solace and placidity. We may "be" that example or we may contribute to the conflict and disruption. Leo Buscaglia, Ph.D., refers to our choices and direction as a river. "We can decide to flow with the river, and live in peace and joy and love, or we can decide to battle it, and live in agony and despair. But the river doesn't care. In either case, all of our streams run into the same sea."

Peace frames a suspension bridge, but exactly what are we suspending over or bridging a space between? The Celtic Night Prayer delivers the answer.

The divine bridge erected is that which ...
a soul in love with God
builds across the dark,
frightening gullies of its
own mind, the strange
chasms of temptations,
the depthless precipices
of its own fears that
impede its way to God ...
He is for whom we search.

Come.

Day 88:   BEAVER

The very powers of darkness are paralyzed by prayer. No wonder satan tries to keep our minds fussy in active work till we cannot think to pray. Oswald Chambers

THE BUTTERFLY COMETH

Beavers seem to be constantly busy working. They gnaw down trees, build dams and construct homes for themselves. Hence, a person who is hardworking is referred to as being "busy as a beaver."

Being busy and productive are positive attributes, but when we are too busy, we lose courtesy for the current minute. We juggle and juggle and juggle—attempting to shift, adapt and modify time. "Trying to alter the moment steals it from us," say Fran and Louis Cox in A Conscious Life. They further sign that if we want fruitful change in our lives, we have to move through each phase, experience its wholeness, savor what it has to offer, notice where we are stuck, and in the process maintain an intimate contact with our most inner sense of self.

Time is not ours to invent and manipulate. It is already here and stands still for no one. Author David White reflects in Crossing The Unknown Sea how we erroneously categorize time. "We speak continually of 'saving' time, but time in its richness is most often lost to us when we are busy without relief. We speak of 'stealing' time as if it no longer belonged to us. We speak of 'needing' time as if it wasn't around us already in every moment. We want to 'make' time for ourselves as if it were in our power to do so. Time is the conversation with absence and visitation, the frontier between ourselves and those we love; the hours become ripe with happening only when we are attentive, patient, and present."

My soul mate, Richie, wrote me a beautiful passage about time. He stresses its importance as a precious commodity, as it is so limited and comes without a price tag. Sharing with you his sentiments ...

Time doesn't look back. Time doesn't yield for the screaming sirens of an ambulance. Time—you can't buy it; borrow it. You can't cheat it; steal it. And you definitely can't change it.

We can remember, though ...

Remember the time your dad helped you ride a bike. Remember the time you had your first kiss. Remember how star struck you were when the only thing you noticed was how her smile lit up the room and how her eyes made you feel safe—pulling you in. Remember the good times and remember the bad times.

DIANA LOUISE WEBB

As we get older, we wish we could take back some of the times—the time we wasted, but we can't. We now know time is a soldier. It marches on. Time is like a majestic bird. It flies by.

Don't waste time arguing with the ones you love. Cherish them because love is a gift from above.

Make friends with time. Take time to meditate. Take time to care. Take time to respect time.

<u>Day 89</u>:   SKUNK

Smell the cheese often so you know when it is getting old. <u>Who Moved My Cheese</u>, *Spencer Johnson, M.D.*

Almost everyone recognizes the odor associated with the small black and white furry animal known as the skunk. The unpleasant smell comes from a substance the skunk sprays at an adversary, but only after signaling an admonition by snarling and stomping his front feet.

Life works just the opposite. It can really reek without advance warning. At such a rank point, it is then that we need to practice tolerance rather than demand it. "Stomp your feet and go for it!" is not an appropriate mindset.

Amid the fusty odor, E. E. Cummings schools us with a hospitable approach to freshening up our nasal passages: "I thank God for this most amazing day; for the leaping greenly spirits of trees and a blue true dream of sky; and for everything which is natural, which is infinite, which is yes."

Every minute of life represents an opening to make "today" incredible—regardless of how it started out. Whether we're in the front row or in the grandstands, today is a truly fabulous moment in time.

Life is good. And life is good because God is good. We are all in it together.

<u>Day 90</u>:   IGUANA

I know in my cells that prayer permeates a sick body, makes it shimmer as the new life comes in, making the cells remember how to respond to the harmonic whole. <u>Bone</u>, *Marion Woodman*

THE BUTTERFLY COMETH

At a veterinary clinic, the doctor was treating an iguana for a bacterial infection. "Little Iggy," hand-carried from Central America, lay motionless under a blanket. His green body turned a pale shade of yellow. About four feet long, most of it his tail, Iggy curled up on the examination table. The cute lizard patiently awaited treatment so he could bounce back to his friendly self. Implementing a natural remedy, the vet felt that remaining close to God and nature would be more beneficial than established synthetic medication and modern techniques.

Sometimes, things just "are." At those times, such as during an illness or even when we are just not feeling well, we have to be forward-looking to realize that the state in which we find ourselves is temporary. We either get well or we die. If we have the faith of a mustard seed, when we think something is "Fait Accompli,"[13] the Lord shows His omnipotent power, even in death.

Modern medicine is an important part of the Western World, but the last chapter of the book does not close just because the medicine cabinet does. It is still "He" whose hands perform.

Day 91:   DOLPHIN

What we have here is a failure to communicate. Strother Martin in Cool Hand Luke

As a contestant in a national beauty competition, I was granted the privilege of swimming with dolphins. The pageant itself took place in the Bahamas. The setting shone with peaceful elegance. During free time, various activities were offered, including sharing an afternoon with a group of friendly sea mammals—none other than the dolphins. I remember their slick torpedo-shaped bodies propelling through the water with such agility. They would jump high in the air encompassing the natural style of a perfectly choreographed routine.

As I latched onto a fin of one of the dolphins, its sleekness of oscillating flippers moved like greased lightning. We were off! Tail

---

[13] A done deal.

swinging from side to side, we glided—bobsledders contending for the gold in Albertville.

Dolphins have been graced with a genetic communication system. Referred to as "echolocation," this sonar structure helps dolphins detect objects in their path. It is their dispatch network.

Humans also have communication circuitry. But unlike our water friends, we normally subject ourselves to a surge of our electric fields. Somewhere there is a jam in our circuit boards and the current does not flow through our wires. In fact, switches often get crossed and the entire setup goes haywire.

Communication is the foundation of any relationship—personal or business. Due to rejection, shyness, not relishing an argument, lack of interest or lack of energy, we don't communicate as effectively as we could or should. Release is one way to see through to a solution. By releasing what we associate with why we don't express ourselves may be the only way to express ourselves. This may sound complex, but emotional and mental frustrations are far-worse demons.

When we hold back our genuine feelings and true thoughts, there is a lack of communication because one party to the conversation or exchange is not conveying clearly. This deficiency of "shutting down" leads to resentment and bafflement. Just like in a game of chess, the players eventually reach "stalemate." Once there is a deadlock of "no budging," both participants have lost. When you allow the current to siphon off, it will be snuffed out. The nebulous raven will arrive and cast a long shadow overhead. You will live in the valley of death for the rest of your life.

Don't become a "lost" participant. Talk about what is ambiguous or bothersome. Be open and that openness will be acknowledged with openness.

Reflection: Has your circuitry shut down?

<u>Day 92</u>:   BEAR

Hug (hŭg) n. An affectionate clasp or embrace. (Webster's New College Dictionary, 1995)

THE BUTTERFLY COMETH

Distinguished by their strong and powerful grip, bears inspire the pet name "bear hug" to signify a hearty squeeze. Gideon Wurdz intimated the definition of a hug as "a roundabout way of expressing emotion." By touching and holding one another, we nourish a need to show we care. That's the joy of living.

"Hugs are good, they feel nice and if you don't believe it, try it," speak the pages of the book, <u>Living, Loving and Learning</u>. We must go beyond just 'being.' "We've got to get in touch with <u>being human</u> and there's a difference."

God has seen to it that our essentials are already within us. When we quit expecting more, we will gain the insight that we already have everything. The rest is up to us to express God's love with others.

Go give somebody a "big" bear hug. Then, give yourself one, too.

<u>Day 93</u>:   LOVEBIRDS

Every man's life is a fairy tale written by God's finger. Hans Christian Anderson

Lovebirds are small, colorful parrots, named for the snuggling shown between mates. Akin to lovebirds, we wish to be loved, caressed and ultimately, we wish to enter into a fulfilling marriage with the right partner.

Marriages these days seem to carry a discrepancy between the ideas we formulate about marriage and actual married life. Marriage is never perfect. What we strive for is to make it "perfect" for us. When we don't reach perfection, we wonder where we went wrong: why aren't we blissfully happy—the image portrayed by movies, the media and "how to love" manuals.

Sometimes we look for love in all the wrong places and for all the wrong reasons. Marriages won't work if they are based on convenience, physical attraction, a meal ticket or someone to get us out of debt. Selecting a spouse by the make of car driven or type of occupation will be nothing other than a brief, vacuous affair.

Love is not time's fool. The unfulfillment delivered shortly after such an encounter will soon birth its own split-up as no base lies beneath the instant gratification to sustain a marriage. As a nail can be driven out by the strength of another object, a new lover can replace a former one just as quickly.

Fifty years ago, the sacrifices made between husband and wife established a bond that no man could break. The dedication remained unsurpassed.

Anne Applebaum, Pulitzer Prize winning author of <u>Gulag</u>, considers the compromises people made "back then" to survive. She concludes that the concessions alone should force those of us living in a luckier era to think harder about what we mean by 'morality.'

Immorality destroys any hallmark of being loved, caressed and ultimately entering into a fulfilling marriage. Our decisions emanate from the passions of the way we think. Those passions work like an invisible seat of consciousness. Our mind, a mental workshop, provides a cognitive component so we can think about what we are doing and why we are doing it. When the pipeline between our passions and our mind gums up, we lose unity with self. Interminably, we putrefy. We retain no values to share with others. We become walking iceboxes—cold, mechanical and emotionless.

Thought for the day: Wise up before you hook up.

<u>Day 94</u>:   MONKEY

Patience is not the ability to wait, but the ability to keep a good attitude while waiting. Joyce Meyer

Ranked among the most intelligent of animals, monkeys are a lively favorite—both at the zoo and in the wild. Able to adapt to almost any environment, they may live for forty years.

Monkeys are mischievous by nature. Hence, the concept has attached itself to human behavior and adopted the label "monkey business" for those who exhibit impishness and foolish antics.

There is nothing wrong with being playfully silly, but there are confines which must be respected. A suitable occasion and place abide for everything: a time to work and a time to amuse oneself. When we cannot discern the difference, those with whom we interact, grow weary and impatient. The calluses of life roughen. The attention span shortens. Annoyance blacktops our smooth cobblestone. Our indecisiveness propagates a languid mind—one which fills with junky thoughts akin to spilled coffee permeating every striation of a linen tablecloth.

"Monkey business" may be revamped into love through the doorway of service. Benjamin Creme is a staunch proponent of "…service of whatever kind, distances you from yourself. As your service grows, expands outward from yourself, you do not lose touch with yourself, but you become less and less concerned with your own ego, your personality expression. Service is the impulse of the soul, the carrying out of soul purpose."

It starts in the mind. Since the mind is a combat zone, the war is a process of elimination—one that requires patience. The enemy is after our thoughts—out to break us down. However, if we can whip the glove of mental sparring in our heads, we can replace devilish thoughts, opposing cortexes of the brain and "monkey business" with meaningful tasks based on love. Man can only run an emotional minefield for so long. When conflict magnifies, we become tired and weak.

Since the business of life is living, remove the monkey from your important business and put him back into the zoo. Just as the monkey is a lively favorite there, be a lively favorite, too. Realign your cortexes with <u>There is a Season</u> written by Joan Chittister. Joan writes, "I finally come to know that my work is God's work, unfinished by God because God meant it to be finished by me."

Finish God's work. Then romp and make merry.

Day 95: STARFISH

To affirm life is to deepen, to make more inward, and to exalt the will to live. Albert Schweitzer

An old fable told of a little boy combing the Pacific seashore after a storm. The low tide left thousands of starfish marooned in the sand. The spiny-skinned sea animals searched with the tip of their arm-like extensions for water. Although not true fish, starfish cannot survive outside of water.

The youngster picked up the starfish, one by one, and threw each back into the ocean. An elderly man strolled by providing advice for a cause which he saw as a futile effort. "Son, there are so many stranded. What you are doing won't make a difference." The child, cradling a tiny five-pointed star replied, "It matters to this one." He then gently tossed the starfish into the crystal ocean.

In the breath of dawn, when you separate the wheat from the chaff, what truly matters ...

A blanket of snow falling in Yosemite. Roses in December. Ink pens full of tubes of ink. Electric garage door openers. Babies' toes. Batteries. Catsup in little packets. Big fluffy towels. Mornings. A full tank of gas. Putting a smile on anyone's face. Watchmakers. Barbecued chicken wings. Pianos. Service of any kind. Vanilla candles. Vanilla cookies. Vanilla coffee beans. A spare tire. Angels. Four-ply toilet tissue. An empty clothes hamper. Trust, honesty, forgiveness. Steam flowing from a piping hot apple pie. True love. Electric blankets on high. Outdoor weightlifting in an early May breeze. Indoor plumbing in winter. Lamps—all sizes. Goldfish. A piece of gum. Sharing a moment brushing hair. Doors. Boots in a snowstorm. The touch of a freshly-lotioned hand. Rain. The elderly. Shakespeare's plays—all of them. Silence. Saying "I'm sorry." Meaning it. Well water. The change of seasons. Memories. House slippers. Chocolate milk in crystal goblets. Multi-colored yarn. The North Star. All stars. Family. The sound of a babbling brook in autumn. Mother Teresa. All mothers. Cuddling in flannel PJs. Shrimp—all kinds prepared all ways. Twisted bows on newly-wrapped presents. Sticky little fingers playing in finger-paint. Making that special person glow. Space. Telephones. Kittens and puppies. Languages. A conscious effort. Miracles. The Miracle Worker. Straws—all shapes and sizes. Seas horses, sea gulls, sea lilies, sea lions, seaplanes and seashells. Hours, minutes, seconds ...

Go make magnificence!

Day 96:   BULBUL

Sit loosely in the saddle of life. Robert Louis Stevenson

A tropical songbird whose natural habitat is found in Africa and southern Asia, the bulbul offers up the most beautiful songs. Granting that the bulbul's feathers host dull colors of brown and

THE BUTTERFLY COMETH

grey, its singing extols so much more—almost like a reimbursement of nature from one area to another.

As mortals, we are born of the earth, nourished by the earth and healed by the earth, tenders Thomas Berry in <u>Making Peace</u>. He presents that in the vastness of the sea and in the snow-covered mountains, insightful stimuli are offered for our art. In the rivers flowing through the valleys and in the serenity of the landscape, perception, whether optical or auditory, is fathered for our music. In the foreboding of the great storms which sweep over the land, intuitiveness is prompted for our ballet. Individually and communally, these benefits are conferred upon us by God's privilege.

As you feel the wind against your breast, watch a new leaf unfurl, listen to the faint serenade of a songbird, or taste the fruits of the season, understand that it is here that life is in full radiance.

Take care of the blessing.

<u>Day 97</u>:   GOAT

I was angry with my friend; I was told my wrath, my wrath did end. I was angry with my foe; I told it not, my wrath did grow. William Blake

Billy the goat lives across the pasture. Clumsy and primitive, Billy commonly runs into the barn door and trips over his own hooves. On other days, Billy seems to take on an entirely different style. He portrays a loving pet—amiable and refined. Still, yet, he takes on a third personality—tetchy.

"How odd," I thought. However, it parallels human behavior. One of the puzzles of loving alliances between loving people is that when everything is super, we still find ourselves acting in unloving ways. John Gray's book <u>Men Are From Mars, Women Are From Venus</u>, assesses the anomaly from a practical viewpoint. It reassures us that this shift, while confusing, is widespread. Dr. Gray explains, "… Two people who are madly in love one day … hate each other or fight the very next day."

Often times, we are suppressing something inside. It could be from days ago or years ago. We then take it out on those closest to us when a trigger kicks into action.

In the beginning of our affections, we may not be as sensitive as later on when love opens us up. We know not our true self except through love. Sharing God's very marrow, we capitalize on our inalienable right to happiness. Yes, we must pursue it, but it is there—ours for the taking. Whether we shout it from the mountaintop or down in the cellar, it is in us and we are in it—all year round. To keep it, we must give it away. Love never fails when we activate the process.

Today, keep love alive. Be attentive. Be understanding. Empathize. Be outrageous. Do it with panache. Most importantly, do it together.

Day 98:   DUCK

The first problem for all of us, men and women, is not to learn, but to unlearn. Gloria Steinem

Peking duck—one of my favorite Chinese dishes. When I vacationed in Portland, I ate lunch each day with my friend, Juanita, at Chin's Restaurant. We loved it. Juanita and I talked for hours while feasting on Peking duck and fried won tons. Of course, no meal is complete without hot and sour soup.

I haven't been back to Oregon for a while, but Juanita is still a terrific friend. She finds good in everything. When I undertook a task or accomplished a goal, Juanita thought it was a "magnum opus." No matter what I did; no matter how poorly I performed, in Juanita's eyes I was a shining star. To me, she's an angel. Juanita's world always glows. As long as she wakes up in the morning, the rest makes for marvelous history.

There are many angels on earth. The sad part is that we erect a soundproof studio around ourselves, impenetrable to our living angels. We brush off the idea that the island of life is made up of more than just self.

In George Maloney's book, That Your Joy May Be Complete, the author endorses that "Angels show their love for God through service of other creatures, just as we are enjoined to show our love for God by serving one another. Angels make God's goodness concrete, both in this life and the life to come."

When we take that moment of reflection and the time to be thankful, we are served with a gourmet plate of meaningful fruits. We can then go back to doing the cooking instead of being half-baked.

The Grocer will tell us to which aisle to go. We must do the rest ourselves…

Day 99:   POSSUM

How bitter a thing it is to look into happiness through another man's eyes! As You Like It, *William Shakespeare*

In the dense underbrush of Australia lives the fuzzy mammal, the possum. He is a member of the marsupial family and has quite interesting characteristics. As a defense mechanism, the possum moves about in the wee hours of the night and sleeps during the day. He has the innate ability to lay lifeless in the company of a predator, taking on the appearance of death.

At one time or another, we, too, have played "possum"—sometimes on purpose; other times, not by conscious volition. Either way, although alive on the outside, we have died on the inside. Something obscures the light of our soul from shining through.

Hildegard of Bingen delineates that "the soul is the greening life force of the flesh, for the body grows and prospers through her, just as the earth becomes fruitful when it is moistened. The soul humidifies the body so it does not dry out, just like the rain which soaks into the earth."

Many things can deaden our spirit—among them, guilt and shame. At these significant times, we must remember we have the right stuff to uplift the soul just like the morning sun uplifts the dewdrops.

"Struggling souls catch light from other souls who are fully lit and willing to show it," fortifies Clarissa Pinkola-Estes. "If you would help to calm the tumult, this is one of the strongest things you can do."

DIANA LOUISE WEBB

Take the time to quiet a soul. Do so united in one truth, one body, one dimension of holiness.

Day 100:   OCTOPUS

A letter is a treat with no strings attached. Alexandra Stoddard

In tropical seas throughout the world lurks the most advanced of all mollusks—the octopus. Calling home a crevice deep in the rocky secretive bottom, this eight-armed creature feasts on lobsters and clams. When in danger, the octopus sprays black ink messages that he will not be taken without a fight.

As humans, we have a need to send messages, too. And what better way to do it than through spraying ink to paper. In Alexandra Stoddard's book, <u>The Gift of a Letter</u>, we may read that a written communication serves our overwhelming need to share, to connect and to feel understood. But sometimes, a letter can deeply hurt. At least once in our lifetime, we have all sent a letter which, in retrospect, we prayed would never get to its destination or the receiver would inadvertently throw it away. We all have read letters that we wished would have been lost in the mail and never reached us.

Whether by 'Pony Express,' fax or e-mail, the universal idea is that correspondence conveys a variety of emotions which may be difficult to disclose in a face-to-face conversation. That is why we are more "open" with our words in a letter. When we don't have to face another person, we can express ourselves more thoroughly and more honestly. Moreover, we are not put on the spot by being obligated to an instantaneous response. We are able to process and clarify that which may not be otherwise grasped.

However, a written message is a permanent message. That message is ingrained in another person forever. Words can and do hurt, more so in written form, as we tend to reread them over and over and over again. Sometimes, we need to be reminded of the fine line between honesty and cruelty.

What is the true color of your ink? What spray are you jetting?

THE BUTTERFLY COMETH

<u>Day 101</u>:   SERPENT

That little word 'but' is the difference between success and failure. Henry Ford said, "I'm going to invent the automobile," and Arthur T. Flanken said, "But ...". Sgt. Ernie Bilko

In the marionette version of the opera, <u>The Magic Flute</u>, three women confront the serpent. The dragon-like creature moves about dangling from strings controlled by a puppeteer. Without the puppet master, the marionette would crumble in an inoperative heap. The doll is lifeless without its lead.

We unwittingly portray ourselves as puppets. God gave us brains and ability; yet, we rehearse excuses to whitewash using our gifts. Our greatest defense technique upon which we rely is the catchall phrase, "…but God will take care of it."

God did not create us to be passive beings of comfort. God helps those who help themselves. For instance, when a light bulb goes out in a lamp, do we just stand there and pray, "Let there be light." Of course not. We have the lead. It has been there all the time. We go into the pantry and get a new light bulb.

God wants us to resurrect our thinking. Recall that Jesus passed through His wrappings on the third day. They collapsed as opposed to coming unbound. His sacrifice placed Him at the right-hand of the Father. This is symbolic in that Jesus wills you to do the same—to pass through what is cuffing you, as you lie collapsed in a heap just like a puppet.

In life, keep the marionette on the stage and not in the live performance, but keep the Master close at heart and hand. You will then rise up one day and take your place with the Father in His royal priesthood.

<u>Day 102</u>:   PIG

You've gotta have support and learn to live daily with faith and humility. Charlie Sheen

The characterization of Wilbur, the pig, in <u>Charlotte's Web</u>, paints a portrait of limitless love which won the hearts of millions.

However, the pig in society is not held in high esteem. On the contrary, the pig denotes sloppiness of personal habits and over-indulging.

We are a nation that loves to eat. We enjoy our cuisine so immensely, we have a nationwide holiday where we stuff food into other food. But eating and nourishment in and of itself does not inspire special meaning. The mealtimes we set aside with family and friends are opportunities to share in quality time with one another.

<u>Pearl's Secret</u>, by Neil Henry, awakens us to the notion that it doesn't matter what kind of china we dine on or what our kitchen looks like; what counts most is how we treat those we love.

The food that unquestionably nourishes us comes in the form of friendship and love. The greatest love is that which is expanded on by Christian analyst, Alice Laffey, who sows that we need God's own divine nurturance to guide us to trust in the 'Author of Creation.'

The next time you go to the grocery store with a forklift, break new ground and fill your cart with three bags of unconditional love. Pick up a two-liter bottle of time prioritizor. Buy a box of willingness. Load up on a few jugs of good cheer. Cash in your recyclable cans of rebellion and rejection which isolate you from loved ones and social gatherings.

Put the "overs" back on the shelf. These include over-eating, over-working, over-spending and over-sleeping. With a balanced diet in hand, zip through the Express Lane in the company of self-assurance, spruced up presentation and tidy order. Hurry back to your abode and open the canister of God's graces. Let the only hunger felt be a rich yearning to complete your home with an obliging heart.

<u>Day 103</u>:   SEA CRUSTACEAN

There is a great deal of unmapped country within us. George Eliot

Crabs and lobsters interlope into our dreams from the depths of our unconscious. Sea crustaceans represent the more rudimentary and crude forms of life; therefore, depicting our unformed ideas and undeveloped drawings.

THE BUTTERFLY COMETH

Introverted and reclusive, crabs progress sideways which denotes thinking on a lateral plane or avoiding an unpleasant task or thought. It is human nature to dodge the repugnant or painful. It may even reach the point where we need to detach. Detaching doesn't mean we don't care. It means we love ourselves enough to stop launching anarchy and pandemonium in both our own minds and in our environment.

When we help others, but hurt ourselves in the process, we live in an unhealthy atmosphere. For any situation to become a gradual grim tango with death is lethal. We must learn to gain and maintain control of our lives. We will never master everything there is to know and we cannot resist downpours, but we can roll with what life sends us and respond accordingly in an appropriate and safe manner. If the lessons involve disarming our hearts and separating from that which is not working for us, we will learn to cope with the pain.

Jacquelyn Mitchard refreshes our thinking to believe in the afterglow of a protracted relationship. This relationship does not have to represent a traditional bond, but may include interaction with self, habitat or natural forces. Mitchard draws a likeness of such parting to that of a fading orb. Bearing affinity to the light of a star that keeps pulsating visibly to the earth long after the star itself has been extinguished, let the tiny scintillating sparkle pave the way to rebirth. It may not make all of your wishes come true, but it enables you to see the light, an energizing nurturing light. This glow illuminates the path to a healthy future—one free of self-actualized chaos and topsy-turvy bedlam.

Day 104:   EARWIG

God's speaking to you. You just don't have a listening ear. Brian Meyers

Named for the mistaken belief that it enters the ear of a sleeping person, the earwig reveals itself with a hard, shiny body and a large pair of pincers. An insect approximately one-quarter inch in length, the earwig commonly inhabits warmer climates. Although it destroys fruits and flowers, it serves farmers by eating caterpillars and snails.

Harmless to man, the earwig may be found relaxing under a stone or decayed bark in a tree.

The paradoxical name makes us wonder how many times we have worn wigs over our ears to enable us to selectively take in only that which we choose to hear. Sometimes what we need to hear the most, we barricade with our wigs—either because it is uncomfortably realistic or it goes against the grain of our plans. Usually at this crossroad, God steps in.

T. D. Jakes, the founder of the Potter's House in Dallas, Texas, speaks of how God allows a problem to arise in our lives so that He can show His presence amidst the difficulty. If the trouble never badgered us, we would not see God's presence the way we see it now.

I met a woman convicted of accessory to the murder of a man she was dating. She invited him over for dinner and asked him to go into the basement to retrieve several heavy computers. He agreed and was met instead by three young men who beat him to death over an unpaid debt.

The deceased's daughter spoke at the woman's sentencing hearing. Her comments set forth that her father would never return from the grave so it was only appropriate that the defendant should never come out of prison. But by making the request for a life sentence, was she vindicated of her anger?

Undoubtedly, the daughter had a right to be angry. She had a right to feel grievous pain. However, does bringing more harm and hurt to a situation ever solve anything? When we run out of virtue, we get desperate. We are the first to appeal for mercy, but the last to dispense it. What we commonly forget in the thinking process, or the emotions which follow or vice versa, is that the road to Heaven is very narrow and that we enter single file.

Perhaps the situation referenced was a test of faith. James 1:2-3 proclaims, "My friends, be glad, even if you have a lot of trouble, you know that you learn to endure by having your faith tested." God knows what we need. When we try to override His plan and do not listen, He gives us plights that humble us so that we will put our trust in Him.

But we do have clout. The same blood which runs chilling cold while impregnated with revenge, can be converted into warmth adorning our veins. "The power is in the blood," according to Bishop

THE BUTTERFLY COMETH

T. Garrott Benjamin. "It's not in the White House; it's not in the State House; it's not in the Courthouse." The power is in the blood of the lamb.

There is always a place to turn to, so that we may be at peace within. Any goulash can be remedied by the love of our Father. He is there to lift us up when the enemy wants to take us under.

Remember, Jesus shed His blood for each one of us.

Let the vengeance be mine. Deuteronomy 32:35

Day 105:   KITTEN

Words—the dress of thoughts; which should no more be presented in rags, tatters, and dirt, than your person should. Lord Chesterfield

Easygoing and reserved, the kitten faintly purrs signifying that she is happy. Silence conveys her message far better than anything else possibly could. "Silence is one of the great and eloquent arts of conversation," asserted Thomas Moore.

When we behold silence, we inherit expression on an undisturbed plane. Engrossed in spirituality, we discover where the beloved take shelter. From <u>Reflections on Simplicity</u>, chronicler, Elaine Prevalle, douses us with a wing of conversance, "Our society plays very loose with words, with talk; yet there is little silence, and silence is where meaning comes from."

Freshen up with silence. Sample the root of reticence. Quench your yen with quiet tidings. Take a drink of silence.

Day 106:   PARROT

Truth will always be truth, regardless of disbelief, lack of understanding, or ignorance. W. Clement Stone

Brightly colored with a hooked bill, the parrot is a sociable bird found chiefly in the tropics. Although highly regarded for its ability to talk, the concept is a bit of a misnomer. Parrots actually mimic words and phrases. They don't create a vocabulary themselves like human beings do. We have the ability to speak and to say anything which comes to mind; but with the gift of speech comes the unspoken obligation to speak the truth.

Doris Klein instills upon us in <u>Journey of the Soul</u> that "true integrity grows from an awareness that we can stand in the honest light of God's unconditional love and be seen in our truth."

So what happens when we are unable to live our truth? We undergo a rude awakening of repercussions. Our spiritual FedEx number changes and our rewards are marked as "undeliverable." When we are the cause of interference, God does not reroute our mail.

Just as a parrot accurately repeats what it hears, we must make sure that throughout our shimmer of time we, too, live and repeat the truth. We should not have to be reminded but once of the ken articulated by Laurens van der Post's statement, "It is the truth that we deny which so tenderly and forgivingly picks up the fragments and puts them together again. We have to be utterly broken before we can realize that it is impossible to better the truth."

Don't wait until death to live truth. Then, it is too late. If we form ourselves so far removed outside of truth and of the image of God, then we will be met at the entrance of the Heavenly cathedral with the words, "I don't know you."

Be not lost to the world and afterlife. Exalt truth.

<u>Day 107</u>:   FROG

Love is the opposite of fear. Love is that fire that does not destroy us, whereas fear is the fire that burns everything it touches. Don Miguel Ruiz

"It was the best of times, it was the worst of times." Those prolific words open the classic novel, <u>A Tale of Two Cities</u>, by Charles Dickens. Although set in the eighteenth century, we are experiencing similar periods now. Day in and day out, we live great lives. But as a whole, our world lives within many disasters and hardships, in part because we don't respect our land and its resources. Regardless, man tries to explain this away.

For example, ancient philosophers offered up that the reason earthquakes occur is due to a giant frog holding the world on its back. When the frog would shift and strain under the heavy load, the earth would move and shake.

Man's prehistoric thinking has since been replaced. Earthquakes are caused by a sudden breaking of a large section of the earth's outer shell. Some scientists hypothesize that when we abuse the environment, we lay the groundwork for the earth's plates to disintegrate, substantially weakening the outer shell. Such abuse evidences itself in the exploitation of world resources and the polluting of our air and water with damaging chemicals.

Nonetheless, we should not fear a premature demise. The healing of the wilderness falls in alignment with God's perfect plan. Nature speaks to us, but it is up to us to accept the dispatch. When we fear the uncertainties of life and not acknowledge the unfavorable in stride, we are not receiving the dispatch.

These feelings take a toll on our cardiac health. It should not come as a surprise that emotions affect the heart. Worried and fearful people are more prone to heart attacks than individuals who are not under such stressors. The damage continues to procreate.

According to Dr. George W. Crile, "We fear not only in our minds, but in our hearts, brains, and viscera, that whatever the cause of fear and worry, the effect can always be noted in the cells, tissues, and organs of the body."

Parallel to how toxins contaminate the environment and foster ruin, deadly nightshades defile the human body and advance sickness and disease. Infested with Black Death, we will never make it to the shining city on the hill.

Stop the cycle before it escalates. Walk on things that used to sink. Let "Be not afraid," dwell within evidencing faith in the risen Christ.

Yahweh, I know you are near.

Day 108:   CHICKEN

Concentrate and you will radiate. Zarlenga

Nothing unusual, just a typical day. George, our bantam rooster, crowed signaling dawn. Dad fed the chickens. The revived fragrance of hay spread across the horizon while the sun peeped from behind its cozy curtain window anxious to start a new day. The desolation of night sought shelter.

As new light found a fissure through which to make known its omnipresent influence, it was suddenly visible that an intruder had crept into the henhouse. The chicken scratches corroborated that a beastly rumpus occurred during the night. Overshadowed by foreign imprints, the coup was in distress.

While the unwelcome visitor left his mark, we leave a unique footpath wherever we go by which others identify us. Our trail may be a spoor of joy, laugher and smiles or it may be a trail of tears and hostility. Our deeds shape our reputation. Between the world and ourselves, we are empowered to cultivate bliss or misery. Our actions can help another person annul the dusk or can cause death on the spot by pushing the individual over the edge.

"No man is an island," claimed John Donne. God created it so. We need others and others need us. To let our return in life sauté in the grease of surly petulance only burns the fowl. We never know what the next person is going through and sometimes we don't know what we are going through ourselves.

The next time you enter a room, take note of the ambiance you set off which lingers about. Are those vibes the footpath by which you wish to be identified?

Day 109:   DOBERMAN PINSCHER

You can't fool the people all the time. Abraham Lincoln

Originally named after the German tax collector, Ludwig Dobermann, the Doberman pinscher is recognized for his "guard dog" abilities. In the 1800s, Ludwig bred the species for protection while making his unpopular collection bouts. Especially ferocious, the Doberman is paramount in shielding and defending; thus, living up to the label as "man's best friend" for protection of his owner. Nevertheless, no matter how close dog is to man, the Doberman has been known to unexpectedly turn on his master.

We, too, have betrayed a friend at least once and have become an undercover anaconda. No one knows what throbbing within causes pulling a Judas. At the very kernel of our existence, we are pure. It is the swaying and coaxing which spoil us. But what is it that thrusts us over the border into double-crossing and two-faced smears?

Obviously, we know our stab in the back will bleed a river of treachery, but we do it anyway. What's missing is goodness. When goodness replaces that which is faulty, a funeral for our venom commences. The malevolent thoughts of our garret are discarded. Our conscience fires up a medley of love and allegiance. But if we choose to build a coffin anyway, we better build two.

Observation: Are you hammering in a nail or are you helping to pry one out? With every slam of the mallet, be reminded that you are breaking trust on the ultimate Friend.

What you did to the least of my brethren, you did it to me. Matthew 25:40

Day 110:   DEER

You've got to do your own growing, no matter how tall your grandfather was. Irish Proverb

A most serene vision is to watch playful deer drink from a brook. A mother diligently safeguards her fawn until the little one is old enough to venture out on her own. Fawns may stay under their mother's wing for more than a year.

One of the hardest moments in our lives is the time when our children reach the stage to venture out into their own world. We long to ensure they don't make mistakes and we try to take away their pain, but we realize we must let go and allow them to experience life for themselves.

Children believe in the perfection of earth. They cannot comprehend devastation, personal loss, famine, or war. Since their needs are met, they assume everyone else's needs are met as well. Behind the innocent gullibility lie answers of practical truth. My friend's eight-year-old son was asked in a contest, "How do you decide whom to marry?" He answered, "You have to find someone who likes to BBQ, who makes sure you have clean socks in your drawer and extra cookie dough in the freezer." Ah, if only the dating game were that uncomplicated. We always tend to complicate life.

One-half of our brain keeps us steady; the other keeps us guessing. The separation diverges year after year, paying out a certainty factor of only one-half. Lack of certainty leads to lack of hope.

Our children are today's future and we provide them with perspectives and perceptions of the world. We pass on what we know as present reality. Pay close attention to these precious investments that will be the future of all things to come.

History has a way of repeating itself. As the past returns through another turnpike, we have to give our children lives that are more principled, more stable and more hopeful than the life which originated with us.

French-Swiss philosopher, Jean-Jacques Rousseau, explained to the civilized world a ticket to happiness: the free development of each child's personality. As good tendencies naturally unfold, parents and caretakers prepare for a harmonious community. "Humans are inherently good," opined Greek logician, Aristotle. Don't let anything demoralize that standing. Forget Jack Frost and become Tom Thumb. Fertilize with love, education, support and deference to God's law. Don't expect reciprocity or improved social circles. "Parent" for the sole purpose of enjoying the most demanding and rewarding job on earth.

Mothers and Fathers, if you reach a point where you want to pull your hair out one strand at a time and holler like Tarzan, take a Calgon bath and then round up the kids for miniature golf.

Tee off with temperance.

Day 111:   BALD EAGLE

No bird soars too high if he soars with his own wings. William Blake

The bald eagle, the nobility of the feathered world, derives its name from white plumes that encircle its crown giving the appearance of baldness. The bald eagle is acknowledged as a courageous hunter. It also represents a proud symbol of freedom as the national bird of the United States.

Admired for its poise, the bald eagle gracefully ascends and peacefully soars across the boundless blue biosphere. A free spirit, the bald eagle harbors no grudges and carries no sadness.

THE BUTTERFLY COMETH

We, too, can be lifted up on eagle's wings when we live a just existence. This means always putting God first. He takes priority before our children, parents and possessions.

My friend, Eva, posed the following dilemma to me: You sister's son desperately needs a kidney transplant. Your daughter is the only suitable organ match. Both children are seven years old. Without the surgery, the little boy would die within the next several months. If allowed by law, would you make the sacrifice of your daughter's kidney?

What a predicament to be in ...

"To love one another as God loves us,"[14] dictates to willingly offer up the kidney without reservation. Buy how many of us would blurt out a hefty "absolutely not?"

When our innate maternal or paternal instinct kicks in, we coddle our child from anything detrimental. The aftereffects of such a concession would be more than most parents could bear.

Now think about what Jesus and His mother went through on the road to Calvary ... . Jesus suffered more than we can imagine. He did so out of selfless choice as He could have stopped the madness at anytime. He died so we could have life.[15]

I didn't have to resolve the answer to Eva's question. I knew the right answer. Then I thought to myself, what if it were my child who needed the transplant or would shortly die? I would beat the pavement relentlessly in search of a donor. If all doors were slammed in my face, I would become inconsolable.

We should never defend a decision based on what we would expect in return if faced with the same situation, yet we do it all the time. We should act solely out of love. Instead, we "coattail" on another's good intentions.

Jesus never rationalizes when He meets our needs and answers our prayers. He acts solely out of love. Whatever we give in love, we will receive during the gathering because nothing in man's world can stop Him who backs our return.

Is your heart ready?

---

[14] John 15:12. "This is my commandment: love one another as I have loved you."
[15] John 3:16. "Yes, God so loved the world that he gave his only Son, that whoever believes in him may not die but may have eternal life.

DIANA LOUISE WEBB

<u>Day 112</u>:   ALBATROSS

It is better to light a candle than to curse the darkness. Eleanor Roosevelt

After it was shot and hung around the Mariner's neck in <u>The Rime of the Ancient Mariner</u>, the albatross brought bad luck. Ever since, this bird epitomizes disgrace, a cross to bear, or guilt.

Helen, one of the ladies in my book club, shared a story with me about a man carrying a heavy cross. He was given the opportunity to trade it in for a lighter one to carry home, for he no longer could bear his weight. Gladly, the man dropped off his onus in the atrium, which was then placed among other crosses in a room. He ventured into a spacious area that spilled over with crosses of all sizes. There were big giant ones which could barely fit under the ceiling. There were huge, heavy, thick ones which stood as sturdy as sequoias. In the far back, a petite little twigged "T" propped itself against the wall hidden by a massive colossus. The man pointed to the small cross and motioned that he would take it. As he entered the foyer to pick it up, he was told the cross was the same one he had originally dropped off.

In life, we are confronted with events which we believe bring sheer trepidation upon us to the extent that we discount what others may be withstanding. We also come to depreciate and devalue the good things in our lives in relation to the crosses we carry. An everyday example is how often we are quick to throw a pity party when we have a flat tire as opposed to being elated that the other three tires are in working order, and that we have a spare one in the trunk.

We are surrounded by blessings. If we dispense ourselves of the albatross, we can appreciate the great love the Father has for us by our recognizing His divine influence.

Take a breather and unload some cargo. Let a fanny pack replace the cumbersome suitcases. Take pleasure in feather-light living!

<u>Day 113</u>:   TIGER

The response of our spirits to beckonings of the eternal ... . George Buttrick

THE BUTTERFLY COMETH

The tiger, charismatic and confident, is portrayed in Chinese astrology as a loner—individualistic, meditative and spiritual. The tiger shuns a chain of command, living a more solitary life which is self-directed and driven from within.

We, the human race, possess our own tiger. Each of us are innovators, trendsetters and individuals—capable and worthy. We need to spot those qualities and make the most of them. Time and time again, life's disappointments have a way of hiding our tiger and chiseling away at our resilience. My wonderful mother once told me, "There will always be disappointments in life. The way we handle them is the art of living responsibly." Ambrose Bierce tagged responsibility as "A detachable burden easily shifted to the shoulders of God, fate, fortune, luck, or one's neighbor."

In the art of responsible living, just think about how great things could be if we peeled away the film from our soul. Unclothed and naked, the soul is forced to face discomfiture. The soul must ascertain creative ways to meet its challenges. It must awaken the tiger to confront the sensations that impede our jollity. Once we are "au fait" with our genuine self, we notice we have worth and can love and accept love freely—not just from one another, but also from God.

Late night: Roast marshmallows, make some s'mores and reawaken the eye of the tiger.

Day 114:   FIREFLY

I look to the future because that's where I'm going to spend the rest of my life. George Burns, U.S. comedian/actor at age 87 (lived to be 100)

Looking out of the back window of my home one evening, I witnessed a gorgeous array of lights. In another part of the country, I would have thought it was the aurora borealis. The golden flashes spread across the meadow like the reflection of the crown of Kilimanjaro. The luminescence that left me marveling turned out to be a band of fireflies.

The firefly, a soft-bodied insect, is also called a "lightening bug" because of the glow it produces on the underside of its abdomen. The heatless radiance is a chemical reaction known as "bioluminescence." Peaceful and attractive, the firefly silently floats through the air.

As a child, I remember dashing about the yard catching fireflies. One of the neighborhood boys and I collected them in jars so we could watch the sparklers in action. But penned up, the fireflies lost their animation. They seemed listless and didn't shimmer, having lost their freedom.

This experience flickered through my mind as I passed a correctional institution on my way home from visiting friends. The facility was located on a dirt road away from the public's view, but I could still vaguely see those incarcerated. The faces resonated a sense of desperation and hopelessness as they clung to the fence. Their orange outfits wavered in a catatonic state. These lost children of a forgotten city likened in kind to the fireflies I captured in my youth. Free, I am sure they beamed with spirit. Locked up, all heart, drive and vitality vanished.

It is also a fact that individuals not behind bars can be imprisoned. The dead-man bones possessed represent a prison of the mind. What binds also builds around the heart. Man can take man out of prison, but only God can take prison out of man.

When we are consumed with contention, the enemy steals our future. God gives us the chance to maximize that future—to bring out every creator gift that has been bestowed upon us. This minimizes our liabilities and we are able to progress forward.

The barrier we come up against is we keep waiting for someone to ride along and set us free. We long for Prince Charming or Cinderella to race on over to our emotional rescue on a white horse or carriage in tow. We yearn for someone—anyone—to drop down and pick up our handkerchief. That isn't going to happen. We need to bend down, pick up our own handkerchief, stand up and press on.

Break the bars, scale down the castle wall and trade your white horse in for a sporty Chrysler. Pop the clutch and fly into a free life.

Day 115:   OWL

Knowledge of the world is only to be acquired out in the world, not in a closet. Lord Chesterfield

THE BUTTERFLY COMETH

Representing advisability and wisdom, the owl greets with great wealth. We each desire the "know-it-all" of the wise old owl. Usually, the only way we acquire such specialized keenness and acuity is by way of the aging process. With age comes judiciousness.

As we get older, we attune to what really matters in life. We see with intelligibility. We distinguish the shallow from that which has depth. What once was a "thinness" in youth now is supplanted with perspicacity.

Seasoning plays a significant role in developing awareness. Still, gaining sagacity is a process. We learn by example or by the school of hard knocks. Profound insight is the brainchild of a ripe mind. To ripen the mind, sketch an outline of that which is gauzed by the sea's breath. The ladder ascends through the mist as we distinguish the slapdash from what is worthy. We cannot afford the luxury of only dangling from the bottom rung.

Once having attained the knowledge to scramble over the sea's breath, ditch your rope ladder. A submarine is now your preferred mode of travel to uncover all that warrants discovery.

Day 116:   BUTTERFLY

I celebrate myself, and sing to myself. Walt Whitman

The most graceful and fragile of the insect family, the butterfly has charmed all for generations. Sporting dynamic shades of blue, yellow, red and orange, it has inspired so many--from artists to poets to philosophers. The ancient Greeks even formed the belief that upon death, the soul leaves the body in the form of a butterfly. They then symbolized the soul as a butterfly-winged maiden named Psyche.

The butterfly dances in the lap of luxury in that she flies light, brings joy, decrees consolation and radiates happiness. The butterfly's ego can be described with a slogan by best-selling author and playwright, Maya Angelou. Dr. Angelou holds that "Life loves to be taken by the lapel and told: 'I'm with you kid. Let's go.'"

Make like the butterfly. Grab life and let's go! Don't watch the adventure. Become it.

He is Risen!

Diana Louise Webb

<u>Day 117</u>:   MULE

Where the willingness is great, the difficulties cannot be great. Machiavelli

In 1989, I spent three weeks at Grand Canyon. It was my first trip to Arizona. Overpowered by the infinite beauty, I was awestruck every step of the downhill hike. Starting at 5:00 a.m., mountain goats plodded from ravine to ravine. An adjoining path led a beaten track of mules carrying thrill seekers with their backpacks. For those who preferred to ride rather than walk the 21-mile round trip, the mules provided warm-hearted hospitality.

Mules remain strong under the harshest of conditions. But when handled lovingly by their owners, mules go above and beyond the call of duty. This doctrine serves humanity equally well. When we employ the Golden Rule by treating others kindly, as we would like to be treated, we bristle with kindness ten times over.

Frequently, we apply a double standard. We demand consideration and bigheartedness; yet we are reserved to repay the same. We feel deserving of work bonuses and lavish presents, but we are not always as giving when the other person is wearing the sandal.

When we share genuine comradeship and a fair exchange with others, we live within an intact medium. Friendly and happy, we are comforted that when we exercise good will towards men, one premonition of the world's greatest thinker, Socrates, comes true. His acumen makes real that "No evil can befall a good man in this life or in the next."

Commit to taking the higher road. Promote the Golden Rule. Practice what you preach. Then, perfect that which you practice.

<u>Day 118</u>:   LION

Life is not a brief candle. It is a splendid torch that I want to make burn as brightly as possible before handing it on to future generations. George Bernard Shaw

Highly respected among animals, the lion rules as server and protector. As King of the Jungle, he assures his kingdom security and sees to it that peace reigns. The thundering roar of the lion re-emphasizes his strength and might. His flowing mane seals his royal appearance.

A lion travels in a pride consisting of approximately 10-35 other lions. The pride lives together like a family. Similar to the lion being crowned King of the Beasts, God wants us to invite Him to be King of our reality. So many of us think we have crowned God King, but actually, we say, "O'kay, God, you can call the shots in the living room and kitchen, but stay out of the loft and cellar." We tend to hide our innermost secrets from others or even from ourselves in our loft and cellar. But we can't hide them from God.

When we do not surrender all to Him, we block a good thing. God can't work when we are lukewarm. Yielding may be a struggle, but with deference comes liberation. And liberty cannot be taken away as its foundation is God.

With lionheartedness, God, I surrender all!

Day 119:   OSTRICH

So, first of all, let me assert my belief that the only thing we have to fear is fear itself. Franklin D. Roosevelt

The world's largest bird is the ostrich. Some ostriches reach eight feet in height. The only bird to have two toes on each foot, the ostrich can boogie up to speeds of 40 mph. Albeit a myth, legend limns that the ostrich puts his head in the sand when tense or frightened. Logic questions what would be found in a sand pile to spark interest as an escape from reality.

In Threads of Time, Peter Brooks cites an experience he happened upon the desert. Brooks climbed over a dune to descend into a deep bowl of sand. There, he crossed paths with a nothingness that was infinitely alive.

When we are afraid or strained, we retreat into the security of ourselves. There, we jot down a perpetual diary, reviewing it over and over about the chapter of concern. Our personal journal may contain helpful avowals or it may billow with useless waste. The dichotomy pulls at each end. Why? Because we spend far too much time on the one hand chasing the dream of the "good life." On the other hand, we fear the nightmare. Nonetheless, dream or nightmare, we are not getting any sleep. We swing like a pendulum. We dread it is the end, but the show must go on. What if we can't go on? Not an option.

As the bandleader of our symphony, we can live as sweetly as Beethoven composed music or we can sour in a royal flop. It is our choice to stand up for our orchestrations and to engineer our own instruments. We can take control of the conductor's wand or we can allow the concerto to play itself. In the latter, as life passes us by, we shadow in vacuity. We lay like a lummox—a simpleton languishing away.

Put the effervescence back into your life by keeping your head out of the sand hummock. Keep reaching for the stars. At curtain call, you will be the standing ovation. Make the encore a performance they won't forget.

<u>Day 120</u>:   BOLL WEEVIL

Both tears and sweat are salty, but they render a different result. Tears will get you sympathy; sweat will get you change. Jesse Jackson

The boll weevil, a wee one-quarter inch beetle, seems far too tiny to wreak the havoc it does in destroying U.S. cotton crops every year. Native to Mexico and Central America, the boll weevil landed on Texas soil in 1890. Although it causes boundless damage by feeding inside of cotton pods, a greater good is also produced. Farmers are compelled to plant different crops besides cotton or they raise farm animals, such as chickens or cows for food. Those new ventures have been even more prosperous than the cotton industry.

From time to time, we, each, have been a boll weevil. We have unleashed seething wrath upon those we love. Whether the indignation surfaces as physical or emotional mistreatment, it is not a pretty sight—just like the ruined cottonseeds. Sometimes being hurt is not visible. While smiling on the outside, our spouses, neighbors, parents, daughters, sons and grandparents may all represent pulverized hearts resulting from suffering inflicted by others.

THE BUTTERFLY COMETH

The next time you have an urge to caterwaul a cruel remark or raise your hand in anger, remember the boll weevil. There is a shot to find another option against which to buttress your fury. A good start is to soften yourself.

Let your senses be enticed by a mingling rendezvous with a bottle of red wine marinade. Enhance the sweet aroma of tenderness.

Day 121:   CRAB

If life is a bowl of cherries, what am I doing in the pits? Erma Bombeck

On the menu, it is a delicacy. Figuratively, the crab connotes a petulant and grouchy person.

Each of us knows of exasperating episodes that we use to justify our "crabby" behavior. We label ourselves as having a "bad day." But is any day truly "bad?" What actually evolves over the standard 24-hour period? My friend, Adrian, elaborates on a decent explanation she heard.

As day breaks, the maiden voyage begins. Freshness fills the air. We are reminded of our favor of sight when we take in the panoramic colors pirouetted by Heaven's glorious lamp.

We indulge in a breakfast piled high with our favorite foods and beverages. Family and friends with whom we are fortunate to break bread surround us.

We then drive to work. We are lucky to have the privilege of paying $4.50 a gallon for gas instead of traveling for weeks in a wagon.

Our job is a place which tells us that we are needed in society; that we matter. Employment gives us a chance to pay our bills and purchase items to increase our comfort. In meeting monetary obligations, we realize we are afforded conventional perks. When we pay the heating bill, we are the recipients of constant warmth and are not left in the street—cold and homeless. Our electric bill cues us in that even under the most dismal of circumstances, we can always live in the light. The water bill confesses that we are favored not to have to haul well water five miles uphill or bathe in a bucket as our forefathers did.

We fellowship at lunch and again at the evening meal, dining with loved ones.

We watch TV, listen to the radio, play DVDs and CDs, talk on the phone and communicate by e-mail. Generations past would have loved to revel in such extravagance, even for one day.

We relax on a cozy couch, splash around in a posh bubble bath and burrow in flannel PJs in a toasty bed with crisp linens. As night falls, we smell the aroma of chestnuts roasting by an open fire. The sunset glistens to spur our consciousness that we are invited to develop reminiscences of our activities of the day.

In the minds of so many, our sunup to dusk forms only an unattainable dream. But truth tells us we are all aboard the same ark. When our boat turns bottom-side up and we are launched into God knows what, it does not have to be a perpetual disaster. A wide-angled scope of walking in faith ladens us with comfort to deal. Without forcing justifications, whatever is transpiring will ultimately be good for us even though it appears to be catastrophic. When we shift our attention from what has happened to what we can do to make every moment count, we live in the big picture and are not suffocated by a cropped frame.

We have the prerogative to choose to wake up "crabby" or pleasantly greet the day. In the rise and shine process, while ruminating on what type of day we are going to have, let us not edit out the inevitable. While we immerse ourselves in amber rays through our curtain at the dawn's early light, there are those who never woke up to see such a glorious new day.

If you can't live it for yourself, live it for them.

Day 122:   BEETLE

I am like the "Cream to Cappuccino"—always rising to the top, even after being shaken. Je'van O. Silvers, Brooklyn, N. Y.

Have you ever wondered how a beetle walks on the ceiling? In addition to infinitesimal claws, a beetle is equipped with adhesive pads on its feet and secretes a sticky substance which functions as glue. Hence, it may hang upside-down literally "sticking" to any surface.

THE BUTTERFLY COMETH

When a beetle becomes "unglued," it falls. But what happens to us when we become unglued?

That all depends on how we deal with the three Cs: 1) Commitment; 2) Control; and, 3) Challenge. Commitment is our resiliency—our ability to bounce back and not give up. Control is how strongly we believe in ourselves and our confidence in being. Challenge is to what degree of success we can make the best of a bad situation or any situation.

We create our own reality. When we concentrate on "making it" instead of how we've been sabotaged, we "uncreate" what we don't want. The longer we carry our suitcases, the heavier they get. Decisions are too important to leave to chance. When we believe in ourselves, our resources become unlimited because we can allocate them effectively. We learn to use what we have to "make it."

A great package for living hinges not on how well we master the good times, but on how well we master the roller coasters. Robert Browning tells us that looking "downward ... makes us dizzy." When we glance upward, we focus with intelligibility.

One by one, we count our blessings as they are showered upon us. These showers drain off the accumulated dirt which causes the beetle inside of us to lose its footing and plunge into a sombrous hush-hush.

As a goal for this season, thwart the urge to become unglued. Regroup the Cs of your life. With conviction, be the cream of the Cappuccino!

Day 123:   SLOTH

If you wait until the wind and the weather are just right, you will never plant anything and never harvest anything. Ecclesiastes 1:4

Everyone hopes for it, but it rarely happens: the "ideal" time. Does it exist? The ideal time to get married; the ideal time to purchase a home; the ideal time to have a baby; the ideal time to change careers; the ideal time to take a vacation.

Realistically, if we wait for the "ideal" time, it will never arrive. In waiting, our lives parallel that of the sloth. The sloth has a blunt nose with peg-like teeth, no tail and rudimentary ears. Grey, coarse hair sheathes its body and long arms and legs. It moves at an inordinately sluggish pace. Introverted, it hangs from branches so securely; it sleeps in the same position. It may even remain hanging in a tree for several days after it dies. Needing very little food, the sloth's metabolism rate is almost comatose. It wines and dines on leaves and twigs, seldom coming down to the ground.

If we live life in the mode that "any more laid back, we would be a corpse," we only advance proportionately to an expired body. As a lifeless form, we deteriorate. If we don't get a move on things, we will solidify in freshly cemented shoes.

The "ideal" time is now. Bolt to the door of life. You've got a job to do. That job is to enjoy living. Make it happen!

Day 124:   PRAYING MANTIS

You shake man han', you no shake him heart. Bahamian proverb

The praying mantis is an insect that lives in warm climates. Because she usually holds her front legs as if in prayer, she is self-styled the "praying mantis." This insect resembles the color and formation of the plant on which she lounges. Her stance creates an illusion of relaxation and friendliness for her fellow crew. However, the praying mantis can be quite vicious—seizing small frogs and devouring her own mate. Depending on whose side we bear witness to, the impression greatly differs.

The mantis likens in kind to the human being. What we see in a person on the surface is not always the true essence of what lives within. To see with precision, we may strip the shellac off a glossed over image by implementing three steps outlined by M. Basil Pennington in <u>Bernard of Clairvaux</u>. We are brought to the first step by reason as we judge ourselves. We consummate the endeavor through the toil of humility. Compassion brings us to the second step. The mercy we grant others reveals deep feelings of our own humanness. These sentiments arise naturally when we are the authentic self. Our previous resistance to helping out is halted and our weapons are laid down.

We, thus, sample the third step—purity in its simplest form. We are swept up to the sight of things invisible. God's heart and our

THE BUTTERFLY COMETH

heart beat as one, creating a constant living intersection through which only good can pass.

What passes through your intersection?

Day 125:   WOLF

Keep your face in the sunshine and you cannot see the shadow.
Helen Keller

It was the fall of '75. I remember it as if it were yesterday. Eight at the time, I went camping with my friend, Jennifer. But this was no ordinary camping trip; it was an exquisite adventure—right into the depths of Jennifer's parents' garage.

We pitched a tent, a woolen blanket draped over a clothesline. We anchored it on one side to a car door and to a freezer handle on the other. Bricks kept the edges of our pioneered wickiup fanned out.

Turning off the lights, we quickly clambered to find our flashlight. The garage fared far more ominous than our indoor bedrooms. Tucked under the covers, we listened to the faint chirping of crickets and watched as a mouse occasionally scampered across the floor. Spiders sought to share our shelter and a family of ladybugs moved into one of our brick moorings.

All of a sudden, a screeching sound infiltrated our abode. We sprang two feet into the air and skedaddled into the house.

The earsplitting yelp was that of a young timber wolf howling at the moon. We darted for more pleasing quarters, but the moon kept on shining.

When people howl at us, are we like the moon? Do we keep on shining? Or do we choose to scowl and buy into the negativity?

Caroline Myss in <u>Sacred Contracts</u> does an excellent job of detailing the boomerang effect of being a decent person in an indecent situation. Caroline writes, "Choice is your greatest power ... even a greater power than love, because you must first choose to be a loving person."

Life will always be stocked with howlers. Among this medley of occupants, Kenneth Wapnick urges us to be a source of love. He cites, "To become a teacher of Love, we need only be willing to hear

Love's Voice and no other. Our responsibility is to let fear and guilt be undone in us, so that this Voice is clear within us."

In a world where the greatest kindness survives the most unspeakable torture, if we listen with ears which only hear the best, we can work beyond the nocturnal white noise of consciousness. We can be a catalyst for the love of creation—with quintessence and quality.

Day 126:   APPALOOSA

We need to reach the end of our rope, then we discover that which is there waiting for us. It is a holy, powerful moment. Arthur LeClair

The Indians were expert horsemen, which enabled them to effectuate successful ambushes on the white man. Frequenting the backs of the most popular horse in the Indian culture, the appaloosa, the Indians proved quick and light-footed.

It was the Spanish adventurers who first brought the appaloosa to North America. The Nez Perce bred the horse about the Palouse River territory from which the name "appaloosa" was derived.

But whether on horse or on foot, the conflicts between the Indians and the white settlers sired savage massacres. Competing interests culminated in blood baths. The Battle of Little Bighorn is the most recognized of all the Indian wars. General George Custer ordered an attack on an Indian camp situated along Little Bighorn River. Under the direction of Crazy Horse and Sitting Bull, the Indians retorted and killed over 250 soldiers in Custer's Seventh Cavalry, including Custer himself. This massive bloodshed is also referred to as "Custer's Last Stand."

In the overall aftermath, was anything accomplished? Are we a better people because of the Battle of Little Big Horn?

When we fall between antithetical dichotomies, either of the mind or in the physical sphere, we suffer internal carnage. Our bodies wallow in pessimism and cynical confusion. Sometimes we need to wipe out our entire selves so that goodness can inflate our bleeding veins.

When we discharge, deliverance penetrates our body systems. Like a recharged battery, we are enlivened with the grace that is constantly born and reborn in us. It is then that we can make life on earth a little more like Heaven.

Day 127:   EUGLENA

In matters of style, swim with the current; in matters of principle, stand like a rock. Thomas Jefferson

At the supermarket on Thursday afternoon, a little girl tapped me on the arm. "I want to ask you a question," she said. Speaking with assertiveness, the child inquired, "Do you believe blind people dream and, if so, what do they see?"

I found myself perplexed. For if a person never knew sight, what would he or she envision?

With big, brown eyes gazing up at me in anticipation, I responded, "I imagine anyone can dream, even the blind. They may not be able to see with their eyes, but they can feel with their hands and understand the composition of objects by touch. As blind people tenderly shape things with their fingers, a likeness is created in their minds. Their hearts give life to the image."

The youngster smiled and pranced off to find her mother.

After completing my shopping, I pondered the question some more. I realize that blind people are no different than those who can see; they only possess more willpower to accomplish a mission.

Recall some of the most monumental feats in history. Individuals under various constraints overcame great problems; they just had to reach under the ordinary to pull out the extraordinary. These people refused to surrender their tenacity. Instead, they worked harder to attain a goal because they had to shape it with their hearts when biological differences changed the way they went about achieving an end.

This story should make us all the more grateful for our good health and create a willingness to show our gratitude by using what we have. In reality, do we do that?

It appears the converse takes place. The healthier we are, the more we add nonessentials to life and the more nonreactive we become. We lose our resolve.

Diana Louise Webb

Consider the purchase of a bulbous, oversized chair and a gigantic big screen television with a remote that does everything. All we do is relax and let the mechanisms think for us and act for us. The more we are removed from our bare self, the more backed up in a superficial casing we become. So overloaded with robotics, the gadgets disable us more than any disability would do.

We are creatures of comfort. We acquiesce in inertness by being too dependent on our "stuff." We then find determination and perseverance unnecessary because complacency has filtered into our bloodstream—scuffling furtively about and overrunning our fundamental constitution until we are worn out, defunct, void of emotion and not caring about any of it.

What we want to do is wake up in this lifetime with a sentience of our bare human characteristics. We may then spontaneously release pizzazz and zing to use what we have in its simplest form.

Examine the existence of the euglena, a microscopic one-celled organism. The euglena glides about in fresh water using only a flagellum, a string-like tail, to change locations. It gets its energy from the sun. This being is idyllically happy as it twirls through its modest homestead.

When we are able to live in a modest homestead, our frugal expectations will produce infinite happiness—and so will life.

Day 128:   SIAMESE CAT

Money talks and often just says, "Good-bye." Proverb

Poised in all her prestige, the Siamese cat symbolizes the Mrs. Howells of the pet world. A universal favorite, the Siamese is independent, intelligent and dignified. She makes a wonderful companion because she is nurturing, giving and generous with her owner. Such love begets love.

When we offer our hearts, pocketbooks and time, the intrinsic rewards are incalculable. But when we squander and keep all to ourselves, we soon find what we have loses its attractiveness and we are miserable. We end up wasting everything because our selfishness and hoarding cause us to enshrine it all and not share. Alone, there is no delight.

THE BUTTERFLY COMETH

We may also swing in the other direction and circle the drain until we are insolvent from misspending. Demonstrating no appreciation for our property and resources, we are soon without.

Be like the Siamese cat. Take pleasure in being independent, but share interdependence—a mutual giving and receiving to refine the sweetness of life. Exhibit self-confidence, but don't hold your nose so high that you can no longer sense the core of heart-opening ephemeral moments. Share out of love and not out of keeping up self-important appearances. Give your finest fruits and not the leftover castoffs.

This week put together a care basket for a homeless shelter. Call five friends and ask them to do the same. This will make all the difference in the months to come—a prompt of how to live and love just a little bit better.

Day 129:   BLUE HERON

The only true joy on earth is to escape from the prison of our own false self, and enter by Love into union with the Life who dwells and sings within the essence of every creature and in the core of our own souls. Thomas Merton

The blue heron is one of God's graceful creatures. It labors through the sky with unique distinction. Its long, pointed bill and striking slender neck add to the features that make this bird the largest American heron. A proud, spirited fowl, the blue heron strides in stately style—alone.

People, like birds, sometimes find favor in standing alone. But being alone too much can give birth to loneliness. Our society has many lonely people. All are human beings who deserve to be treated as worthy individuals and not as isolated dolts. No one should ever have to feel lonely and left out. All men have value. More often than not, we don't apply value to those in forgotten domains.

A poignant account by Pastor Bill Yount of Mount Hope Ministry best illustrates this point.

"It was late and I was tired, wanting to go to sleep, but God wanted to talk. It was about midnight, but it dawned on me that God does not sleep. His question made me restless. 'Bill, where on earth does man keep his most priceless treasures and valuables?'

I said, 'Lord, usually these treasures like gold, silver, and diamonds and precious jewels are kept locked up somewhere out of sight usually with guards and security to keep them under lock and key.'

God spoke, 'Like man, my most valuable treasures on earth are also locked up.'

I then saw Jesus standing in front of seemingly thousands of prisons and jails."

Forgotten vessels have a calling that lies dormant when we neglect and banish them from our current reality.

Pastor Yount concluded his story with a message we each would be the wiser to mind.

"The Lord said, 'If my people want to know where they are needed, tell them in the STREETS, the HOSPITALS, the MISSIONS, and in PRISONS. When they come there they will find me and the next move of my spirit, and they will be judged by my word in Matthew 25:42: For I was hungry and you gave me no meat; I was thirsty and you gave me no drink; I was a stranger, and you took me not in; naked and you clothed me not; sick and in prison and you visited me not.'"

If you choose to restore the forgotten people to God's House, there will be victory and rejoicing. If not, are you prepared for the consequences?

Day 130:   SHREW

I may be in the gutter, but at least I'm looking up at the stars. Oscar Wilde

The shrew is among the smallest of all animals—weighing as little as a penny. It resembles a mouse with a long pointy nose and whiskers. Shrews pose no danger to the human race. They feast on insects and grub, usually living near marshes and streams.

When we think of a "shrew," this animal is not what comes to mind. What we picture is a cranky, nagging individual who finds fault with everything. The law that brings another into his or her life is the same law by which that person is held there. If we are glum, we attract people who are also glum. Unless joy is poured onto the combo, our sponge will remain drenched with vinegar.

To test whether or not you have fallen under the spell of the "shrew," capture the words as they spew from your mouth. If they are too uncouth or too gruff, they will prick like a thorn. If you feel such a pierce, unveil the activity of God within you.

This activity is love. As love attracts love, your sponge will rinse with abundance beyond your wildest dreams. Elect to unwind in love.

Soak.

Day 131:   ROADRUNNER

For where two or three are gathered together in My name, I am there in the midst of them. Matthew 18:20

Ground-dwelling and swift, the roadrunner races through the deserts of the southwestern U.S. speeding past the parched thistles into an asylum of brush.

When we congregate in the name of Jesus, we experience a safe place just as welcoming as the safe hideaway of the roadrunner.

Our shelter is a holy place—a temple where we gather as brothers and sisters in worship. This joint service of thanking, praising and glorifying procreates great power. In unity, prayers are answered, friends consoled and enemies' disputes resolved.

Led faithfully within a team of believers, our life journey becomes our life dream. Walking hand-in-hand with one another in God's presence, we are colored in the profound awareness of His creation.

Today, ask someone to pray with you.

Day 132:   COMMON BLACKDEVIL DEEP-SEA ANGLER

I'd rather die on my feet than beg on my knees. Marva N. Collins

Far-reaching into unfathomable waters live some of the most unusual fish. Acquainted with science by name only because of their cavernous location, these creatures are described as having captivating large eyes with teeth just as big.

The common blackdevil deep-sea angler is a deep-ocean fish that never surfaces. Measuring a wee 3½ inches long, this species of angler resides in the lowest abyss of the ocean. At that level, the water is cold and black.

We have all undergone cold and black times. One which is by far the darkest is a reality check of where we may possibly go if we died tonight ... Perhaps a loaded question, but a sensible one. Sometimes, we get so caught up in living, we forget the road to hell is paved with good intentions. Blinded by not just the blings in life, but the trifles, the propensity to slip into cold and black times invades our being as we are seduced by sinfulness. If we can remove that aspect as the focus of our existence, we grasp a higher level of value for ethics upon which to live a normal life.

Finding delight in the commonplace of living, we keep abreast of a cognizance for joy reaching out and expressing itself everywhere. We come to appreciate this simple richness in everything from folding laundry hot from the dryer to sharing a taxi. We can even see the beauty in the "cold and black," including our new friend, the common blackdevil deep-sea angler.

Day 133:   LAUGHING KOOKABURRA

Laugh and the world laughs with you. Weep and you weep alone. Poet, Ella Wheeler

Found nesting in tree holes in the woodlands of Australia and New Guinea, the laughing kookaburra lives true to its name. This animated brown and white-feathered bird received its handle from calling sounds, which simulate laughter.

Laughing is a contagious antidote for most of what ails us. From the pressures of life to clogged arteries, a good, sincere, deep, cheerful laugh adds life to our years.

According to Dr. Michael Miller at the University of Maryland School of Medicine, watching fifteen minutes of a comical video increases blood flow and relaxes the peripheral arteries for up to forty-five minutes. When we laugh, we forget our worries and become a radiating center of God's peace.

At issue is that we don't seem to laugh enough. Caught up in "the world," we rebuff that a laugh can tickle us. Its self-helping charge and air of amusement are far more therapeutic than the most satisfying aperitif. A giggle turns teardrops of desolation into resurrected droplets of holy, living water.

Extend the length of your lifeline. With optimism, connect robust cardiovascular fitness and emotional energetic health with an exuberant and chipper laugh. If you need a paradigm to follow, envision what it was like when Christ laughed ...

Day 134:   SHEEP

I'd like to make a motion that we face reality. Bob Newhart

A shepherd has a very unique vocation. He tends to his flock with equal care for each of his sheep. He discerns where his drove is at all times. He sees what the sheep do and ushers them away from what they should not be doing.

Just like a shepherd knows his sheep, we know ourselves—sometimes too well. We claim to be catering to what is in our best interest, but is that interest from our ego's agenda, or is it from what is genuinely called for in order to live a respectable and long life?

Humans chase a "high." We engage in extreme sports, life threatening kicks and take crazy chances. Why? Because we believe "it" will never happen to us. We become scofflaw kings. We try to beat the yellow traffic light, function without sleep, go home from bars with people we don't know, don't wear a safety belt, smoke the wrong plant and take one for the road.

The indisputable truth is that "it" happens to all—rich and poor, black and white, strong and weak, honorable and scandalous. No one can avoid "it." Sooner or later, "it" catches us. But if we live right, we can go "later" rather than "sooner."

Notwithstanding that God has a decent scenario for our lives, we may cut the splendor short. That is why it is important to make well-informed decisions and to be cautious in the things we do and in the ways we live. Acting on impulse has lost its trend.

DIANA LOUISE WEBB

When we purposely or carelessly err, the maelstrom of life sucks us into a descending helix. As we fall into the funereal black hole of helplessness, we are out of options.

"It" has arrived—ready or not.

Day 135:   PUG

Spiritual longing is a sort of loneliness for an unknown yet deeply perceived presence. Some call the presence God; some call it peace; some call it consciousness; some call it love. The Seeker's Guide, *Elizabeth Lesser*

My friend, Lori, owns the cutest toy dog. Sparky Doodle, a pug, romps and plays as if he were the master of his palace. Just shy of ten pounds, Sparky Doodle spoons with Lori at night for a nuzzling siesta. His short, smooth hair and wrinkled face adorn security and restfulness when nestled up to Lori. The reciprocated show of fondness beams from the owner's face.

But what is it like to reach around and only find emptiness? This void may be symbolic of a broken heart. Our hearts are broken when relationships end, dreams fade or we grieve over a loss.

Author Thomas Lynch writes about heartbreak in Undertaking: Life Studies From The Dismal Trade. He asserts that, "Heartbreak is an invisible affliction. No limp comes with it, no evident scar. No sticker is issued that guarantees good parking or easy access. (But) The heart is broken all the same. The soul festers. The wound untreated can be terminal."

Mourning is romance in reverse and if we love, we grieve, and there are no exceptions. We must then stand on the shoulders of the faithful. As life awakens its hidden wholeness, we are strengthened until we can once again stand on our own two feet.

Meditation: Is your faith strong enough for others to stand on your shoulders?

Day 136:   TURTLE

The aim of an argument or discussion should be progress, not victory. Joseph Joubert

THE BUTTERFLY COMETH

Slow-moving and unaggressive, turtles have existed for the last 200 million years. Even though their speed would appear to be a detriment, closer inquisition reveals that even at the most lagging pace, turtles keep moving. Nesting in the mud of tall grasses, turtles make no haste. Careful in their kickstart, they think before they advance.

We live in a society that is not like the world of turtles. We are quick to anger; quick to act. We have quick tongues which send quick cutting messages. We don't slow down to try to annul a burden instead of being one. We steer ourselves toward the redress of injustice—but only on a personal level which affects us. In our hunt, we seek revenge as a quick fix-all. But is it? Confucius says, "If you devote your life to seeking revenge, first dig two graves."

This day, raise yourself to the degree of sanctity for which you are destined. Slow down. Fold your animosity and ill will. Nest in righteousness. Nest.

Day 137:   SEAHORSE

Give a warm hug to one next to you because that is the only treasure you can give with your heart and it doesn't cost a cent. George Carlin

Ahhh… the beauty of a saltwater aquarium. On a larger scale, the Great Barrier Reef offers divers a sea of aquatic life in a tropical fantasy wonderland.

I think everyone has a favorite sea animal; mine—the seahorse. I remember the love and camaraderie shared by a group of baby seahorses in Queensland, Australia. Resembling tiny horses performing Tchaikovsky's Nutcracker ballet, I longed to stop time just to savor the spectacular production.

We all wish at one time or another for life to stand still: to behold a special moment, to avoid a disaster, to gain more minutes to make a decision, to catch a biting insult.

In the days of Joshua, Joshua prayed to the Lord to prevail upon the sun and make it stand still. Surrounded by the enemy, he feared if night fell, the rivals would overpower. Acknowledging Joshua's appeal, the Most High subdued the sun.[16] The sun stayed and hastened not to go down for approximately one day.[17]

If it were only so unproblematic now to savor time ...

Ironically, it is. God gave us a bonus to enhance time's worth. We are endowed with "memory" to keep any piece of time forever. We are also endowed with tips to help us act in those situations where we wish time would stand still. For example, we are created with nerves and senses to empower us to react in a crisis. We are graced with a thinking cap, giving us the ability to be our own wizard on the spot. We are born with the gift of speech that may just as easily offer kind words as spout off hurtful ones.

We possess other assets which are meant to be shared. These include hugs, the power to sacrifice, having open hearts and the capability of being a friend. Ultimately, our most precious asset is our love.

We may elect to misuse what we are granted or we may employ our assets to fashion the greatest underwater marine show that the earth has ever seen.

Be the aquatic tightrope instead of falling from it. Rather than clowning around, be the merry-andrew and make things nicer for the audience of life. As the fish are swimming through hoops, help your neighbors eliminate their hoops of entanglements. Don't let the ocean elephants charge; you take charge. Last, but not least, as the acrobat swings above the water with zip and spunk, swing through life with an extravaganza at your "Big Top."

Day 138:   CHAMELEON

When wealth is lost, nothing is lost; when health is lost, something is lost; when character is lost, all is lost. Rev. Billy Graham

Ranging from 1¼-25 inches in length, this breed of lizard has the remarkable ability to change colors and adapt to all predicaments. It may be yellow, green or white one minute and change to brown and

---

[16] Joshua 10:12
[17] Joshua 10:13

THE BUTTERFLY COMETH

black the next. The chameleon's color is regulated by its hormones which influence color pigmentation.

How often have we desired to change or hide something about ourselves? Better yet, disappear altogether.

People change their clothes and habits, but character basically remains the same. Mirroring the chameleon as it camouflages itself, we want to conceal our undisciplined traits from onlookers. Lying and hypocrisy come under the umbrella of privacies we don't want revealed outside of ourselves. We prefer to masquerade as riding the white horse.

All of this is unnecessary and draining. If we simply allow ourselves to be ourselves, we will be the people God created. Freed from our Mardi Gras, our muscles and ligaments no longer need to muster up the oomph to continue the entertainment. Our minds are discharged from the duty of a storage shed for our fabrications. George Graham Price helps us remove our frosting in theorizing that as we become interested in the secrets of life, we discover life holds no secrets. The scales of life never balance but on one side.

It's time to put away the costume. Park the impostor in the closet. Gather the strewn pieces of your life that were shredded by double-dealing. Piece by piece, realign.

Now that you can see who you are, "be."

Day 139:   BABIRUSA

Education is what survives when what has been learned has been forgotten. B. F. Skinner

The babirusa, a wild hog found in Indonesia, lays prey to man as the natives heavily hunt it. Its long tusks make it attractive for the kill. Now considered an endangered species, the law protects the babirusa. Poachers still operate on the "black market."

When we acquire illegally, we may get what we want, but the joy is diminished, as there is no Christian pride or reward. Laws are enacted to make life a little nicer for all of us. Laws that protect wildlife are especially important. If we didn't have them, nature would disappear. There would only be buildings, factories and warehouses. Our environment would be polluted; the animal habitat would be destroyed.

Much of the time, we are too preoccupied with gauging our personal lives that it slips our mind we are part of one amazing universe. We fall short in educating ourselves about what is transpiring around us and what we can do to help.

When knowledgeable, we not only develop admiration for the subject matter at hand, but we also are privy to how we can chip in and do our part.

Mount the satellite dish of life in your backyard. Expand the channels. Let your left hand explore the frequencies. Let your right hand synchronize them. Educate. Enlighten. Execute.

Day 140:   ANT

It's the greatest of all advantages to enjoy no advantage at all. Henry David Thoreau

Ants—those little annoying insects that seem to pop up everywhere. But what if ants were medics ... how many lives could be saved?

Sorry to say, ants are not medics and can't save the world—neither can anything else, not even all the money in the Federal Reserve Bank, when our appointment comes.

In 2005, one of the richest men in the world died. Worth a reported $20,000,000,000, John Walton, the son of Wal-Mart founder, the late Sam Walton, lost his life when his homemade aircraft crashed in Wyoming.

It doesn't matter who we are, we live on borrowed time. During our sojourn, we reach a stage where we rationalize our physical being on earth is not forever. Ruminating on our misdeeds, our moral compass decides our need to do something to make it right with the man upstairs so we may enjoy the snug cabana in the beautiful waves of the eternal ocean. In haste, we pull out our wallets and donate our last cent to the church.

Reality check: You can't buy your way into Heaven.

THE BUTTERFLY COMETH

In God's eyes, it matters not from which pulpit you preach or from which holy book you study; it's about your spiritual framework.

I was napping one afternoon when I found myself entranced in a very strange dream. I was walking down an alley with a faceless stranger. We passed a man huddled next to a garbage can. We didn't help the man; we didn't love the man; we did nothing. As I looked back at him, he stood up and opened his hands. Blood spilled from every pore.

I now know the homeless man in my dream was Jesus and we just turned around and kept walking. What a brutal reminder of how ruthlessly we treat each other. When we are remiss of love and overlook the teachings of Jesus, but expect to set the world on fire, we only delude ourselves.

God will not advocate something not created out of love. By denying our fellow man, we remove love from our linear array of daily equations. When that happens, the machete falls.

As the saying goes, "It's not over 'till it's over." Until the last roundup, we can do what is right—not for man, but for God. A blind instinct exercised with nothing more, commonly radiates from a cowardice motive. Following Christian principles involves much more. "A genuine Christian conscience," elaborates Father John Dietzen in Catholic Life In a New Century, "is a product of persevering effort in charity, faith, maturity, reflection, prudence and prayer." The quandary is that those teachings do not always fit in our personal docket.

It will not be until the black camel kneels that man will recognize God's will as He sees it and our consequences for failing not to.

Day 141:   CLOWN FISH

Toto, I've a feeling we're not in Kansas anymore. Dorothy, Wizard of Oz

Noted for their sprightly orange color striped with three blue-white bands, clown fish live among large sea anemones. Swimming in and out of the anemones' tentacles, they remain unharmed by the stingers which may be fatal to other sea life.

DIANA LOUISE WEBB

In their element, these colorful fish are comfortable. Out of their medium, the graceful princesses scatter like a bag of dropped marbles.

When we are on our own stomping grounds, we, too, are comfortable. But when we are yanked from our cushy milieu, there is chaos. This pandemonium can be the result of a sudden move such as mandated in the military or a job or school relocation.

Every single day of life requires adjustment, but it doesn't have to be sheer babel. Meeting a crook in our life's path doesn't advertise a fate of being permanently plucked from our course. As we travel the sand of our hourglass, the lay of the land will never be completely level. With each variation in topography, we come to realize that we don't know the depth of our faith until it is tested. But life isn't constantly a test if we live it as a gift.

So concerned with keeping in our niche, we lose the elbowroom generously provided by God to enjoy something unfastened from our daily setting. He is there to fill up the spaces with His awesome surprises. We need only make a space in our heart for Him to abide and faithfully accept that which He brings is always best for us.

That said and understood, when we are again yanked from our cushy milieu, there will be no chaos; only happiness and comfort. If we happen to hit rocky roads, we are assured God is only across the bend with his tractor and chain.

Day 142:   CHINCHILLA

Here lie I by the chancel door; They put me here because I was poor. The further in, the more you pay; But here lie I, as snug as they. On a tombstone in Devon, England

Indigenous to South America, the chinchilla mainly inhabits Peru, southern Chile and northern Bolivia. Sometimes mistaken for a rabbit, the chinchilla's thick blue-grey pelt is highly valued in making expensive, luxurious coats—some as costly as $99,000.

But whether we own a high-priced chinchilla or a simple faux fur, we stay warm all the same. In the end of times when the chosen are invited to rise higher than the earth, keeping up with the Joneses will not even rank last on the list of all that is cherished.

THE BUTTERFLY COMETH

As the Enterprise is boarded for divine exploration, nothing of man's world will be needed. In fact, nothing will be able to be taken—not coats, no jewels, no food, no clothing, no pictures and no money. God will supply all. He created this world with His almighty words of "Let there be ...". Those powerful words still reign today.

Now and again, we ignore that everything we have comes from God. He giveth ... and He taketh away. We only have because He allows it. If we make a purchase, like a chinchilla fur, it is He who provides the means as well as the animal from which it is made.

There is enough good to go around for each of us. That graciousness will serve those who are humble with contrite hearts. Those who gloat with earthly riches are living their reward. There will be no room for them and their belongings on the Enterprise.

Look at your lifestyle. Will there be room for you on the Enterprise?

Sometimes when I sit silent listening for God, my breath takes on the rhythm of the sea. The rising of my chest becomes the wave forming from the vastness of the sea, that powerful and rounding curve which hungers for the beach rears up until my lungs are gorged on air and still and still my breath must choose to throw itself from off the cliff of will.

Rosemary Morgan
"The Reaching"

ANTICIPATION AND ELATION
FROM A HOSPICE LIFE-CARE CENTER IN ĀGRA, INDIA

Before the butterfly takes on civilization, it must adapt and develop its own style and distinction. The butterfly's traits may be similar in all members of its own species, but it has the opportunity to progress and enhance its own character. Mirroring the butterfly, mankind needs to discover a framework within which to bear the fruits of love, faithfulness, humility and human decency.

Christel wraps up her season volunteering at a hospice life-care center in Āgra, India.

The head of our life-giving influence is Christ. As we form one body in Him, share with Christel the gift of giving back.

- ❖ Tender your hands in service.
- ❖ Come with a heart made for loving.
- ❖ Witness with eyes that only see the best.
- ❖ Lift up the poor and broken with strong and willing arms.
- ❖ Listen with a compassionate ear.
- ❖ Stand with a foundation of personal integrity.
- ❖ Think with an honest and grateful mind.
- ❖ Walk with one shoe on the other foot.
- ❖ Go forth with an immaculate and peaceful soul.

Let the infinite presence of God color your world with love.

Diana Louise Webb

Day 143:   WILL THE FOUNDATION BREAK?

God is the foundation of life. Go build on Him. Lisa Frandsen

Literally speaking, our physical foundation is our framework, the center of which is the spine. Metaphorically speaking, having a spine means to pursue one's convictions while having the courage not to yield to opposition in achieving personal and professional goals.

Resisting forces is difficult to do. Thankfully, we each are blessed with a voice that tells us right from wrong. It bears witness to the obedience of truth in authority to the supreme good to which the human person is drawn. When we are in truth's camp, it appears all combatants are our nemeses.

A classic example is found in the Star Wars saga, <u>Revenge of the Sith</u>. A line of dialogue written eleven years ago struck a universal cord—Darth Vader's contemptuous admonition to Obi-Wan Kenobi, "If you're not with me, you're my enemy."

This is not necessarily true. Siding with principle is part of the search for meaning, a quest that must begin and end with God. Absolutes cannot be defined by man. The verdict of judgment of conscience endures as a pledge of hope and mercy, God speaking.

Life is not a test of virtue; life is solely worthwhile by way of virtue. Our journey is our education, guided by Him who has dominion over our circumstances. If we are distracted from educating ourselves, then suffer we must, more than what is necessary.

Also siding with principle is the realization that there are truths bigger than our earthly ideals. We cannot afford the luxury of believing in an ideological hypothesis, the conclusion of which explains life in black and white terms. These limitations attempt to decipher in a scientific jumble of words what has happened, is happening and will happen in our human community.

The truth is that life is not simple consciousness. The words "simple consciousness" refer to experience, not life. There are higher paragons by which to abide: values of simplicity and humility. That is why we can capitulate ourselves in absolute trust to truth and faithfulness in all things.

THE BUTTERFLY COMETH

There will be those who question whether the planet can thrive without more, suggesting the model is too Pollyannaish and unrealistic—a thinking beyond reach. This is where "backbone" confesses itself, where our moxie comes alive. When our hearts are full, the wealth flows from our mouths: God's prescription for life, faith and hope. The more "Word" we assimilate, the stronger we become, the more sturdy our foundation.

When next asked to take a stand or be a powerless pawn, side firmly with principled structure. Let the jelly remain in the jam jar and not serve as the buckling agent of your backbone. Refuse to be tossed into an indecisive heap.

Look at the face of every decision. We don't always see our contribution beginning and ending with God. Interestingly enough, He knows differently.

Day 144:   GROWING A BEARD

If you want a guarantee, buy a toaster. Clint Eastwood quoted in the Investors Chronicle

Living in the vibrancy of our "spunky years" is a bittersweet sensation. When we remember the "good 'ole days," we chuckle and feel fuzzy inside. This is pleasurable and adds life to our years. In contrast, when we attempt to "become" our past, we are lost in the wake of yesterday and only taste artificially flavored joy. When the past won't die, the future can't live.

If a scientist could discover a formula for recapturing youth, this would immediately gain billions in revenue. But as life stands, we cannot relive the past nor can we stay young forever.

Growing older does not denote a windup of the grand life. It is the natural progression of God's plan which He created. Aging is a golden stretch to reap the benefits of a lifetime of hard work and acquired wisdom procured over the years.

Life, as a whole, is a fantastic adventure. Each stage has its own splendor. To stagnate in one interval of time forfeits humanity's assortment of rare indulgences. Muhammad Ali once so wisely professed, "The man who views the world at fifty the same as he did at twenty has wasted thirty years of his life."

DIANA LOUISE WEBB

As you enter your next shining season, forage lands you know nothing about. Don't look back. Be happy "this moment." It can't be relived, but it can be polished up to gain something for the future.

Time is never overdue for new dreams, renovating current ones and rebuilding aspirations.

Day 145:   EYES

There are none so blind as those who will not see. Dylan Thomas

The eye, a spherical ball of mysticism, has transfixed the medical field for years. The eye enables us to see our surroundings. Sensors in the retina detect light. The cornea and the lens focus the light. Nerve impulses are then sent to the brain.

With the beauty of sight, why is it so often that when we "look," we do not "see?" We are selectively blind to what is crucial. Just as the eye transmits light, we are transmitters of life. The ingenious astuteness of D. H. Laurence imparts that when we fail to transmit life, life fails to circulate through us. 'Give, and it shall be given unto you' is still truth. It means rekindling the life quality that has seeped out. When we close our eyes, we live an indifference which gradually penetrates until we are distanced from a straightforward assessment of the world.

Abide by the tutelage of William Goyem in The House of Breath. Go into the world. Go build cities. Save and join and piece together to form a whole. Gather the broken pieces; connect them. Make like a map, a world where all things are linked together and murmur through each other.

When you awake tomorrow, as you open your eyes, see the world with a mindfulness that expands outward from self. Look more towards opening doors by aiding to piece together and unite all that is on the fritz, disjoined and wounded. May your eyes always serve as "red carpet" portals to the hearts of those crying on the inside.

Rise up in splendor!

Your light has come. The glory of the Lord shines upon you. Isaiah 60:1

THE BUTTERFLY COMETH

Day 146:   FIVE-STAR PORCELAIN VENEERS ON A BONDO DENTAL PLAN

You already have enough bargains you can afford. Julie Haas

Trading in a ski boat for a yacht we'll have to make payments on for the next twenty years doesn't seem like the smartest thing to do, but we have all done it, if only by way of analogy. We chomp off more than we can chew and become frazzled because of it. We take out second mortgages to pay for an inground pool; purchase a new suit, but can't pay the electric bill; or spend the rent money on the latest home furnishings.

Success's real power is not predicated on gathering the most toys. Some of the most successful people who own many things can vouch for this. For instance, Tina Turner references the underlying delight of her happiness with a statement that, "The real power behind whatever success I have now was something I found within myself—something that's in all of us, I think—a little piece of God just waiting to be discovered."

The concept of the "seemingly small pocketbook" arises from our inherent yearning for felicity. When we don't have a bond that grips more than a peripheral stratum, we only know life on a shallow plane. Never seeing anything further in concentration than the cosmetic effect of a cubic zirconia, we crave more—a bigger, better gizmo.

If we fix our attention on giving back as opposed to obsessing about how high to pile our empire, we stand above what we own. Impossibilities become plausible. Happiness takes on a role much greater than the exhaustion associated with keeping up highfalutin garnishes. What we previously construed as a germane deficiency is no longer haunting us. We apply ourselves to making a difference in the world. As we remain faithful to rejoicing in simplicity and altruism, we soon comprehend that what we do have is more than plenty.

By hallowed power, our rusty puddle jumper grooms the streets in top fad. Unsophisticated hedge clippers turn our stark lawn into a sweeping botanical Eden. That old, shabby, black dress hanging in the closet suddenly reveals vintage distinction making us really hip.

Diana Louise Webb

Effectuating a fresh start with a new attitude, we cross the finish line in cutting edge swank.

Now that's truly chic!

Day 147:   ACQUIRING "THE NERVE"

The most sacred place isn't the Church, the Mosque or the Temple, it's the temple of the body. That's where spirit lives. Susan Taylor

We have all been in those agonizing and awkward situations where we must "face the music." Every undertaking begs repercussions. The marvelous grace of being human would lose something in its experience if we were not presented with overdrafts we had written which had to be cashed.

Have you ever wondered where the term "face the music" originated?

There was once an Emperor who enjoyed the enchanting music of a particular flutist. The flutist always performed with an ensemble. Together, the troupe played as beautifully as Mozart composed music.

But deception loomed as the musician never ever blew one note. He piggybacked on the instruments of the other entertainers, solely puffing hot air.

One day, the Emperor called on his favorite music maker to render a solo. Knowing he could not even toot so much as a flat or a sharp, he feigned an illness. No one bought it and the flutist was summoned for a private production. Unable to "face the music," the man committed suicide.

Convening the nerve to bite the aftermath of a gaffe is frightening and stressful. Uncertainty pervades and we fear the unthinkable. At the eleventh hour, it is the fluidity of passage in our conduit to God which gives us the spizzerinctum to uncork the pressure. We can then compose our own concerto and promenade to our own ditty. If we subsequently have to "face the music," we do it with rectitude. The best cure for a sin is Christian love—the song of a humble heart.

This week, grab your flute and toot your own horn!

THE BUTTERFLY COMETH

Day 148:   AN EMPIRE OF REASON

Minds are like parachutes—they function only when open. Proverb

Kendo is the art of Japanese fencing. It is both, a sport insofar as one tries to win competitions, and a martial art insofar as one tries to improve self through martial practice. There are two dimensions to kendo: action and spirituality.

The "action" dimension consists of delivering an effective technique. This is accomplished through the use of a sword or "shinai"—a saber constructed from four pieces of bamboo bound together. The "spiritual" dimension is found in fostering the mental state from which the art originates.

Although kendo appears to be primarily engaging in a sword fight, it is not about muscle power or strength. It is about speed, agility and proper attitude. The technique, to be successful, must be delivered with an "empty mind." To be at such a state of consciousness, we need to learn to void the mind of any thoughts. Thoughts clutter the mind. They keep us invisible from ourselves.

Don't lose "you" because of self-possessed concepts. To do so is to slowly expire. Clear your mind and get rid of the hodgepodge.

Close your eyes. Concentrate on consolidating all of the useless contents in your head in a bundle. Lump together your conclusions, disorder and the mishmash.

Let this giant mass coagulate and then roll right off your back.

You'll appreciate the relief.

Day 149:   INTERNAL SECRETIONS

The greatest kindness survives the most unspeakable torture. Linda Williams

One of the vital body systems without which we could not live is the endocrine system. Responsible for secreting substances directly into the bloodstream, by comparison, we need to be careful what we secrete into society or choose to hold in.

Author Mary Cholmondeley styles this correlation relative to finding contentment. She writes, "Every day I live I am more convinced that the waste of life lies in the love we have not given, the powers we have not used, the selfish prudence that will risk nothing and which, shirking pain, misses happiness as well."

When we suppress, we deteriorate. We "settle." Existing via brainless automation, we thrive without heart. Vis-à-vis, when we disgorge toxins into the public domain, the negative voice is a destructive language and language is an authoritative tool. Language commands growth, happiness and fortune. It can also slash the spirit as sharp as a fillet knife, carving out all that truly matters.

In life, we either make ourselves weak and depleted or we make ourselves strong. The amount of energy is the same. Our path offers us something to learn which leads to greater fulfillment. It is our decision whether to invest the energy. Our energy affects other energy systems. If we emit waves of gloominess, we are sliced off from the universal steam of the world. That steam is love. When we lose love, we lose touch with God's presence, power and grace. We revert to our selfish being—a state from which love takes us away.

Life is too brief to create space for waste. Before you lies another day. Use revitalizing morning energy to secrete your best.

<u>Day 150</u>:   ACHILLES' HEEL

Happiness is not something you experience, it's something you remember. Entertainer Oscar Levant

In Greek mythology, Achilles was the greatest of the Greek warriors in the Trojan War. The Greeks eventually defeated Troy, but in the last year of the hostilities, Achilles refused to continue the battle over the loss of a young-maiden war trophy to another warrior.

Incensed, Achilles spurned further fighting and the Greeks began to fall short without him. Achilles' best friend took his place, but was killed by Hector, the most praised of all the Trojans. Seeking to avenge his comrade's murder, Achilles rejoined the combat, eventually slaying Hector.

Tragically, the recoil of nature consumed Hector's brother, Paris, and he shot a fatal arrow into Achilles' heel, the only part of his body not immunized from harm. This act spawned the metaphor,

THE BUTTERFLY COMETH

"Achilles' heel," as being a vulnerable weakness, a chink in our armor which can cause demise if not protected.

Each one of us has an Achilles' heel. It may be a physical impairment, the impact another has on us, or the influence our own vices exert. It is up to us to guard ourselves from that which is carcinogenic. The billboard messages of our Achilles' heel are ones that constantly appear roadside. We can either read them now or we can read them later. At some point, we have to address them and remedy the vulnerability. On the recovery aspect, it's not always bad news as we have the final word of choice.

Day 151:   LENDING A HAND

Faith and reason are like two wings on which the human spirit rises to the contemplation of truth [and the spirit cannot take flight without both]. Pope John Paul II

In the busyness of everyday life, we could all use another pair of hands.

Fortunately, we have two hands which we were dealt: our earthly existence and the "Great Beyond." Opportunity exists to live forever. In the Gospel according to Mark, Jesus tells us, "Truly, I say to you, there are some standing who shall not taste death before they see the Kingdom of God come with power."[18]

The Risen Lord is going to return. The significance begins with the resurrection of Christ, not His blessed event in the lowly manger in Bethlehem. The birth of Jesus fulfills His destiny as the eternal Supreme Being. The Book of Isaiah prophesizes, "For unto us a child is born, unto us a son is given; and the government shall be upon His shoulder; and His name shall be called Wonderful, Counsellor, and Mighty God, the Everlasting Father, the Prince of Peace."[19]

Christ's promise to come again is our hope and our salvation.

Throughout the conundrums of conflicts and denials, only one light burns and keeps our souls aglow until we reunite on the other side. This light is the King of Kings, the Lord of Lords.

---

[18] Mark 9:1
[19] Isaiah 9:5

Blessed are those who have not seen with their eyes, but believe through faith.[20] They will be the ones who are extended a hand to join in the "Great Beyond."

How do you live the two hands dealt to you?

Day 152:   DON'T PUT YOUR HEART IN A DEEP FREEZE

Take the first step in faith, you don't have to see the whole staircase; just take the first step. Martin Luther King, Jr.

When we run a red light or fail to pay a parking meter, we may easily take care of the problem by forking out funds to the city that issued the citation. Usually, attorneys are helpful in negotiating resolutions of this type.

But life isn't fair. The folks who have the financial means can hire better-skilled lawyers. They readily enjoy hassle-free living devoid of turmoil. But do they really?

Contrary to public belief, money cannot fix all the rasps. It doesn't matter how much moolah we have; it is not an antibiotic for crimes of the heart.

Our inner tabernacle is a host to a plethora of felonies, among them: envy. As our conscience tugs on our mind, we cauterize it. Then we experience a jangle which tears us apart. Being our own jailer, we employ resistance to dissociate. When we can't make the break, envy invades our whole body and takes over.

If you must be a jailer, send out bounty hunters on a search to capture the anima of jollity. Lambaste the scorn and jealousy. When you then appear before the Judge for imposition of sentence, you will break out of the leg irons and push away from the bars that barricade and incarcerate.

Your file will be stamped: parole granted.

It's called "grace."

Day 153:   TONGUE

---

[20] John 20:29

THE BUTTERFLY COMETH

When I was twenty I was in love with words, a wordsmith. I didn't know enough to know when people were letting words get in their way. Now I like the words to disappear, like a transparent curtain.
Wallace Stegner

Paul Williams' book, <u>Critical Lives,</u> features an excerpt on Bangla, an alcoholic concoction made out of the trash dumps of India. This potent mixture is comprised of fermented animal innards. It deadens stimulus reception making it very popular among the street people—the poorest of the poor who have been divested of all human dignity.

Bangla is very cheap to produce inviting mass appeal even though it kills more of the human race in Bengali than malaria.

Tragic as it is, there are communities in our world who believe the quality of life to be so miserable that they knowingly risk death to dull the senses. They are unable to find one morsel of happiness to savor in a 24-hour period. There is nothing in the day which makes life worth living.

We see the same concept on the home field of our affluent nation: gone astray souls suffering from sadness. The painful graphics expose individuals speaking fate with their tongues that they may be delivered from another day of life.

The power of speech is incredible. Asking for something that we may request on a whim may generate unintended results by its grant. To numb life with words of damnation is not giving graciously unto God whatever He takes from us.

Give yourself and you will develop a tongue for what God says by way of your own words. It's a fashioning of God. Just listen.

<u>Day 154</u>:   ANATOMY OF A CELL

Thou hath seen nothing yet. Don Quixote

Cells are the landscaping of the body. We consist of millions of microscopic cells that have specialized roles. Constantly growing, maturing, dying and replenishing themselves, cells keep us alive.

While we are breathing and being active, are we really living?

DIANA LOUISE WEBB

The external landscape is the semblance of internal life. Unhappiness wears its frown on our exterior much like a rust formation's debut on a pristine car fender. The upside is, that suggestive of how cells regenerate, we have the wherewithal to slough off what scorches the eyes and smudges the soul. We are able. Sanctified incandescence dispels any doubt.

When we are open to spiritual intervention, what is a sphere above us appears with crystal clearness to "Lime Away" the corrosion that puts the scowl on our body. Better than botox, our renewal beholds the many faces of a prolific life. We come to understand that life breathes beyond our house and our street.

Each cell of our body serves as a citizen. In conjunction with one another, a great coalition materializes. When we are charitable, when we dole a warm heart and serve with generosity, we are similar to our cell alliance in that, when in unison, our efforts make the world a body of everlasting arms.

You are an heir to the breath of life which carries forth precious promises.

<u>Day 155</u>:   IF THE NAIL BREAKS, THEN ...

Victory is not found in the ease of our circumstances nor in the strength of our resources, but in the presence of the Lord who is with us. Roy Lessin

The human nail is one of the hardest substances of the human body. Nails are actually plates growing from the matrix which is the location where the nail cells divide, lengthening them. The hardness is derived from keratin.

When a nail breaks, it leaves the tip of the finger or toe exposed to the stinging elements until the nail grows and is pushed forward over the nail bed.

When we break "the code," be it the laws of God, nature or social concerns, we, too, expose ourselves to the pain of a very stern system of redress. By not conforming to what is right, eventually our branches will humbly bow in repentance, as wrongdoers never come out on top.

THE BUTTERFLY COMETH

Each break is another crack to our personal integrity, another crevice dividing our character. If we choose the alternative, we embrace a solid constitution. We are no longer competing with the corporal self.

Ernest Holmes points out in <u>Creative Mind and Success</u> that "By conforming our lives and thought to a greater understanding of Law we shall be able to bring into our experience just what we wish, letting go of all that we do not want to experience and taking in the things we desire."

Engendering honesty, credibility and a reputation on the up-and-up, the rancid is catapulted out of our playing field. The showdown is over. We have won the face-off.

When you examine your matrix, what do you find?

<u>Day 156</u>:   OUR DEFENSE MECHANISMS

Lord, may I not so much seek to be consoled as to console; to be understood as to understand; to be loved as to love. St. Francis of Assisi

Anyone reading this book has suffered from "nasopharyngitis," better known as the "common cold." To spar with the illness, our bodies are equipped with unique proteins called antibodies which make up our immune system. When released into the blood, antibodies neutralize infectious agents, enabling us to live free of disease.

As stewards of mankind, we serve as an immune system for our neighbors. When we notice behaviors that make them paltry or create the potential of losing their salvation, out of love, we have a duty to gently persuade them to see a different way to follow.

This does not green-light the temptation to act the role of a detective and search for imperfections, nor does it sanction causing discord for the sheer gratification of tattling. Love is the sole incentive: we love others enough not to leave them where they are when heading for a bad fix. We may not change things, but with tenderness and patience, we have done our job as God's steward.

DIANA LOUISE WEBB

Stewardship is one of the most important things we can offer our community. As our reasonable responsibility to God above, when we get involved out of loving motivation, all else falls into its due place.

Day 157:   THE SIGNS OF LANGUAGE

Ideas shape the course of history. John Maynard Keynes

Life is full of sounds. But picture living in a world without sound. In absolute silence, for a moment, step into the loafers of the auditory-challenged ...

Systems have been developed to allow the deaf to substitute gestural symbols for spoken words. The most universal is sign language. The world of sign language is a separate sphere which has taken on an identity all of its own. This course of development advances premium clues to expanding the vernacular of the hearing impaired.

As part of man's biological heritage, we seek to understand the source of language. An interesting idiosyncrasy is that sign language does not cover grammar, yet those who use it base the symbolizations on solid intuitiveness.

In comparison, the structure of a human being follows suit. We have solid bones and minds from which to develop intuitiveness. We are not mired with trivial disorder unless we set our compass in the wrong direction. Like Jack and his famous beanstalk, we are capable of growing above the fuss that distracts us from our best days. But we have to use it or we lose it. If we don't whet our appetite with ethical scruples, our cravings will be sated with a gorge of junk food. We deprive our bodies of vital nutrients, digesting only empty calories. In the long run, we become ineffective and purposeless.

Pray for a replenishment of your vitamin and mineral reservoirs with living water. Fortified with sustaining armament, you will never be famished or die of starvation. You will live forever as a child of the light—God's special sign language for those who follow His teachings.

THE BUTTERFLY COMETH

<u>Day 158</u>:   YOU ARE THE AIR I BREATHE

In the name of God: Respect, love and serve life, every human life! Only in this direction will you find justice, development, true freedom, peace and happiness! John Paul II

An amazing woman, Dolores, is a great family friend. While going through a troubling time, she was there to remind me that God is always close by to lift me up on eagle's wings.

Dolores' faith never falters and she shared with me a beautiful thought about God being the life air in our lungs—there to supply our needs and to cleanse and restore us.

As it encouraged me, may it so, too, encourage you. Enjoy!

Have you ever experienced seeing a bright sunbeam of light coming through a window in such brilliance that in this "GREAT LIGHT" appear innumerable fast moving particles of dust? In "that" light, can be seen "things" that cannot be seen in normal bright light. These "sunbeams" that expose all of the dust particles aren't visible just any place, nor do they appear to us every day.

One particular day, I was in my family room where I daily spend time in prayer and reading. I was seated where God's sun came through the window with His intensely bright sunbeam. I was startled by the vast amount of dust that I could see floating in that beam of light. I immediately realized how dirty my house was and that I had been totally unaware my family and I were breathing all of this dust into our lungs.

As I was pondering on this, God's still small voice said to me, "This is how your heart looked before you surrendered your life to Me to be your Lord. Little by little, I have been cleaning your soul from the many impurities that have come into you. Some, you were born with through your bloodlines. Some came through violations against you in your childhood. But many impurities are from your own "self" choices. I am the only One who cleans your heart. Only when you come to Me for TRUTH cleaning are those impurities removed. My WORD IS MY TRUTH PURIFIER. You must choose to position yourself in My Sunbeam of Truth."

There is a popular Christian song that goes like this: "You are the air I breathe—Your Holy Presence, living in me." God so loves us that He is always waiting for us to come closer to Him. He is pure Light. His Light reveals darkness. We human beings tend to love darkness more than light because of the many enemies of God who infiltrate this earth. God sent His son to rescue us from the hidden impurities of darkness that are meant to destroy us.

Let Him be the "air you breathe—His Holy Presence—living in you." His Light Love casts out all fear and cleans your heart and lungs, soul and body.

Day 159:   HAIR

You'll be more fulfilled with your hours in the day if you separate the wheat from the tare in the threshing floor of life. Julie Haas

Deb is my hairdresser. I think of her more as a magician than a beautician. Deb can convert a limp and lifeless head of hair into becoming, spiffy tresses with only a few snips with the shears and a quick coif of a comb.

We, too, can be like magicians and convert ourselves into dapper kings and queens with a quick coif of our outlook and disposition. Likening to hair, how well we treat life and the way we care for ourselves will determine the length of our extension.

Paralleling the color we tint our locks to achieve an appealing presence, we color our life with a similar ideology. But sometimes that which we may lay eyes on as a sought-after hue, although on tap, may not wear well. Nonetheless, we choose the color of our indwelling. It is a matter of volition. We may opt to color our world with love or not.

When we opt out of love, we square up against hate and indifference. Imagine spending one day a week being unlovable. That would equal 52 detestable days a year—almost two months. Over a life span of 80 years, more than a straight decade would be dowered with loathing and revulsion—24 hours each day, seven days a week.

Could anything squander more of life's dear resources?

Life is a time to look forward to God showing up each morning. In an uncongenial setting, we are not making that happen. By the same justifiability that we refuse to abide by a less than desirable hairdo, we cannot bear up under vials of scorn.

THE BUTTERFLY COMETH

This morning put on your tailored bon ton and strut. Good hair day or bad hair day, God showed up. Greet Him in the style of love.

Day 160:   CHIN UP

We don't always understand the ways of Almighty God—the crosses sent us, the sacrifices demanded... But we accept with faith and resignation the holy will with no looking back, and we are at peace.
Anonymous

Chin up, but not out. You have a lot for which to be thankful!

A=Amazing graces
B=Best friends
C=Chuckles and smiles
D=Dreams
E=Earth and energy
F=Forgiving hearts
G=Gardens
H=Healing and health
I=Invitations to holiness
J=Joy
K=Kind and neighborly folks
L=Loving, living, learning
M=Miracles
N=Newspapers
O=Occupations and job opportunities
P=Pens and pencils
Q=Quality
R=Running water
S=Seasoned elderly gems
T=Truth
U=Universities and colleges
V=Vision, voice, vocabulary
W=Wildlife
X=X-tra specials greeting cards
Y=Young little tykes
Z=Zany laughter and more laughter

Diana Louise Webb

<u>Day 161</u>:   COVERED IN THE PRECIOUS BLOOD

There would be nothing to frighten you if you refused to be afraid.
Mohandas Gandhi

God's approbation starts with the blood of the Lamb—the washing away of our falls from grace. Cleansing us from all unrighteousness, we are free from Lucifer's clutch.

So why do we walk the walk of life as if hiking across a hilly goat ranch? Why do we deliberately tumble down a slope and give away our rewards?

No force steals our jubilee. We freely relinquish it. The dilemma we face in leaving happiness behind is that we don't trust in our Lord to be there, especially when every choice hurts.

We live in a cash and carry world. In one way or another, we pay. Sometimes we pay a lot and sometimes we pay a little. Sometimes we pay with all we have. In the confusion, we forget someone else has already paid the salvation invoice for us. Hoofing up and down bluffs and dells are foolish ways to spend the days when, instead, we could be enjoying the good life.

A local newspaper reported that a Romanian prisoner filed a lawsuit against God for screwing up his life. The man charged breach of contract as he was serving a 20-year prison sentence and felt the scenario did not coincide with God's promise of the "good life." But whose fault was it?

We, not God, are the ones who turn every day wrong side up one minute at a time. We are the ones who jimmy the plan by changing our flat tires with the wrong ratchet.

Before creation itself, God loved us and it has been in His heart ever since that we live the "good life." By not opening up to the Lord, we forfeit our freedom and joy--the prodigy of the "good life."

But deep down inside where it really matters, in looking back on our lives, we see God at times and in places we previously assumed He wasn't present. By His own blood, He delivered us. He bathed our dead works to sprout new life.

Ransomed with His precious blood, our life is not transitory, but without end. We have it. It is ours. Do you recognize it?

THE BUTTERFLY COMETH

Day 162:   A TIP FROM THE TIBIA

The art of life lies in constant readjustment to our surroundings. Kakuzo Okakiwa

Dynamically spurting in a relatively short period of time, the tibia develops quickly and can turn the shortest youth into a tall drink of water during his adolescence. But physical expansion is only one type of branching out. We spring up every year—sometimes for the best; sometimes for the worst. Gluttony ... Lust ... Pride ... all top the list of motivating triggers that cause us to head south.

No one is born to be evil. We are pure beings. What happens from there lies in "free choice," but rarely do we cold-heartedly wish ill will upon another. It is usually a two-part process: we ferret out a desire and step on the next guy to get it. Inescapably, somebody gets hurt and that person is routinely self. Why? Such question may be best answered by Vietnamese Buddhist monk, Thich Nhat Hanh, who wisely imparted, "When a man spits at the sky, the sky is not sullied. The spit falls back in the face of the one who spat."

Those who try to harm others cannot keep on for the long haul; they only harm themselves, as evil will never triumph. When we get off course and stray from our rock, we fragment and are the ones who imminently turn to dust prematurely. However, with a veer of our pick and chisel, we may once again be northbound with the same unspoiled integrity with which we were born.

God danced the day you were born. Keep the spirit moving.

Day 163:   IN HEBREW, IT'S OUR "KAPH"

You keep looking for the lost key out here on the front lawn because the light is so much better out here. But the truth is, the key is right where it's always been—in the house, in the cave of the heart, in the darkness of night. Joe Zantollo

A physicist once said that if the atoms in the palm of the hand could be released, there would be enough energy to power all the utilities of a city. That fact alone brings forth to the forefront of life the metaphysical power and substance of the human body.

Diana Louise Webb

At the center of the atoms that make up every vein, artery and capillary is light. That light radiates throughout our bodies and discharges its magnificence into our extremities. We can either let the light soothe, caress and create greatness or we can cut it off and inflict pain, block out goodness and cause fretting.

The palm has a matchless quality. Its dexterity denotes a wide range of applications from clapping in applause to touching the mouth as a gesture of love, to waving wildly in desperation. In all cases, the palm is a symbol of strength and empowerment. I never knew to what degree until a life-changing experience passed my way.

While traveling on a bus from Connecticut to Illinois, the driver made a stop in Columbus, Ohio. It was roasting on this June day. The heat combined with the exhaust from the motor coach took its toll. Instead of taking in the charming scenery, all I could manage was a view of the inside of a Greyhound station. Permanently affixed to a squalid metal chair, slugging 7-UP from a bottle wrapped in brown paper, I quickly drew the attention of a forlorn man. Since woe loves a sidekick, he plopped down beside me. He couldn't have been more than twenty-five. The man, very distressed, immediately emptied his personal baggage about how he lost his wallet. It contained all of his identification, his bus ticket and his last twenty dollars. The man's wife left him because of a drinking problem. Now, he found himself being stuck at the bus station. After unloading his disappointments on me, he decided not to board the bus and left the station.

Feeling the need for air myself, I shuffled outside. There wasn't much to see. An overpass sheltered the highway not far from the depot. As I looked off into the distance at the arch, I spotted what appeared to be a man teetering on the adjacent narrow rail of the bridge. It was about a sixty-foot drop to the freeway below. Zoning in, I realized the man was the one with whom I spoke at the terminal.

In retrospect, I sensed his depression, but I didn't comprehend the gravity of his mental anguish. I instinctively ran to the bridge yelling, "No, don't do it!" He looked at me and I directly at him. With an empathetic smile, I edged onto the viaduct. He simply stared and kept repeating, "You don't understand. I've lost my identity. I've lost my life."

THE BUTTERFLY COMETH

I continued to ease further to the rail. I asked the man if we could talk for a little while. He didn't actually agree, but let me know his name was Howard. I had never been confronted with a situation of this nature before and was at a total loss as to what to say or do.

"Howard," I mustered after a moment. "It's no accident I'm on this overpass with you. Everyone else walked to a fast-food restaurant for a bite to eat. Too sick to go, I stayed at the station. But it wasn't my illness that prevented me from going. No, it was God's way of putting me in the right place just for you, at the perfect time when you needed me."

He replied, "Give me a break. Do you really believe God even knows I exist?"

I responded, "Of course, He does. God is chaperoning you every step of your life. He is here. He is the one who made sure we would have this conversation right now. He sent me to help you."

In a leap of faith, I extended my palm toward Heaven as a motion for him to accept the miracle—a sign that life was not his to take, only God's.

Howard gazed at the expressway far below and then looked at the blue sky. Only a few minutes passed, but it seemed like hours. Every movement felt like a slow motion video. Suddenly, Howard placed his life in the palm of my hand. He reached out and as our palms touched, I discovered we could have lit up the city. Defying the skillful trickery of evil, we rediscovered love and hope. Howard's life started anew.

Howard was not the only one who started that day anew. God's calligraphy left an unforgettable mark on my heart. At times, my faith was too faded to see miracles. Whether by arrogance or ignorance, I allowed the ink in the meaning of life's pen to evaporate. I had not lived my own faith as fully as I could have.

Being there for Howard strengthened my belief that we don't need to understand God's ways or what His calendar holds. It is sufficient for us to just know we are included in it.

In a poem by Helen Steiner Rice, "Daily Thoughts for Daily Needs," Helen inscribes, "God never sends the winter without the joy of spring... And though today your heart may 'cry'—tomorrow it will sing!"

In your faith walk, lift your palms skyward to take in the loving energy from God's electric company. Then go out and power all the utilities in your city!

Day 164:   MAKING HEADWAY

Some people succeed because they are 'destined' to, but most people succeed because they are determined. Elmer Towns, seminary professor

In the evenings while writing my book at the reference center, Lori, the librarian who is also my close friend, frequently queried, "Saving the world, today?"

Without waiting for a response, Lori would bring a few pencils to the table along with several sheets of writing paper. Her accommodating workshop was a gracious vestment of God. It churned inspirational ideas upstairs.

Inside our complex, round dome, many great scholars are born—commencing sizzling-off-the-cerebrum new theories and thoughts to make the world a domicile for all God's people.

Ivy Baker Priest talks about our world and its myriad of untapped promises. She writes, "The world is round and the place which may seem like the end may also be the beginning."

With each circle we journey in life, we say hello to new premieres and bid arrivederci to curtains which are due for closing. What we make of the entrances which bare face each day directly affects whether something will be a beginning for us or a last gasping adios. We glean the ability to recognize the variance, the same variance that receives the nod from the depth of God's love for us. In our connection, He wants our endings to be a holy birth—an awakening to more loving and healthy living.

When we reach that abounding affirmation in Christ, the headway to which we aspire will not only be doable, but also never phase out. Our wagon will be permanently hitched to a star.

Zoom on up folks!

THE BUTTERFLY COMETH

Day 165:   BEHIND OUR BACKS

You can tell more about a person by what he says about others than you can by what others say about him. Leo Aikman, writer

Being our real self is an empowering experience in that being a pecksniffian is wearisome. When we feign to be what we are not and then say ugly things behind the backs of our loved ones and friends, we are fatigued. Adding denigration to indignity, since the jab comes to those whom we profess to be proud to call our friends, we keep layering the paint—distorting reality. The new picture of self is a fraud.

Even when we are phonies, and we have all done it, the heart still belongs to God. He sees what is inside, and it is that which is underneath that matters to Him.

We are happier when we are not a people of many faces. The only way out of the corkscrew is up. Transcending over and above the fake ornamental glass house, there is honest-to-goodness genuine life. "Keeping it real" with family and friends, we meet the charge of our purpose—to labor in the Lord's chateau to make the stay better for others. Part of that courtesy is to forego parking a Boeing 747 in the hangar of our ego and resisting the enticement to dredge our neighbor's quarry without regard for what our own mineshaft tailings have deposited.

As you wrap up this sally, lose the air. Cash in the trash and trade up to more prosperous commodities. Find one "face" you like and keep it. Once you make these investments, your dividends will be endless.

Day 166:   WALKING THE GREEN MILE

Whatever else the day may bring, one thing is always true, that God is ever constant, in His love He has for you. Emily Matthews

Barb is a terrific woman. A pier of support and a mainstay of inspiration, she helped me brave some of the rockiest turnpikes in my corniche of life: a 12½-year federal prison sentence.

Diana Louise Webb

Having worn the same sandals, Barb shared with me a moving story about the priceless value of God's love—a love that conquers all barriers and delivers a tenderhearted gesture which becomes its own return. May you be as blessed as you read what Barb relayed to me.

They say it never rains in southern California, but in the spring of 1990, it rained daily during my first year in prison at FCI Pleasanton.

After nine months, I was learning that my needs were simple and could actually fit inside an eighteen-inch locker. Crackers and peanut butter meant freedom from having to eat in a prison cafeteria. One book was sufficient in comparison to the four or five I used to check out from the library when I lived in Kansas. Two blouses and two pairs of pants took me from one laundry day to another. One pair of sneakers worked—until a hole appeared in the bottom of my left shoe. That tiny hole seemed like the last straw, my breaking point in a situation that should have broken me sooner.

I thought back to my journey that led me to this prison cell and, once again, I felt despair. On the outside, I was a suburban housewife married for a dozen years to a man whom I loved dearly and who loved me without question. But I was a woman of many secrets.

My husband never knew about the horrible abuse I endured as a child at the hand of my father. He never knew of the nightly visits or the silence of my mother. Our family was good at keeping secrets and as I was growing up, by all appearances we were a typical middle class family. My husband knew I was uneasy around my dad, but he treated him with respect and even love—spending time fixing up his house, waxing his car.

My father was a great pretender and he certainly had my husband fooled. He fooled everyone and, frankly, in my mind and heart, I wanted nothing more than to believe we were a normal family and that the past never existed. So I kept still about my history and tried desperately to bury the horror.

My father owned a business and after my mother died, he put me 'in charge' of the books—which meant I was to sign any document he put in front of me. Because I was adept at doing without hesitation

THE BUTTERFLY COMETH

anything he asked, it never occurred to me to read or question what he was doing.

When the FBI showed up at my door with my signature in their hand, I had no defense. Once again, dad fooled everyone and in the words of the FBI, someone was going to prison. That person turned out to be me.

The best thing that happened during this horrible time was that the truth finally came out. The secrets were revealed. My husband was suddenly presented with a wife he never knew. My history became public and the shame was almost unbearable. In the process of the investigation, we lost everything—our home, our savings, my reputation and almost our marriage. But my husband, after careful thought, stuck by me and believed in the person he knew I was deep inside, not the person being prosecuted.

When I self-surrendered at FCI Pleasanton, I did not consider that the shoes I was wearing would be the only shoes I owned for the next two years. I would have been better prepared! But my life in the suburbs did not prepare me for life in prison. I had zero street smarts.

There is purity, though, in losing everything—you finally come down to that part of you that cannot be disguised by the stuff of your surroundings. In the outside world, I may have appeared successful, but I was a shell of a woman. My nine months in prison had strengthened me, allowed me to get beyond the chaos in my surroundings and the voice of judgment in my head to the heart of 'who' I truly was. I didn't find Christ in prison. Christ was an old Friend—the only Safe Place I went to during the worst of the abuse as a child. But I did find peace and for the first time, I found integrity.

Then came that little hole in my shoe. Walking to my work detail, I would have cold, wet feet for the rest of the shift. After my sock dried, it would once again get wet going back to my 'home.' Walking to the commissary or the cafeteria left me shivering. The one way I found solace in prison was to walk the track outside—no matter the weather. Now it was simply a reminder in each step how vulnerable my newfound strength really was. It felt like another betrayal.

I couldn't ask my husband for money to buy shoes. He was struggling on the outside trying to rebuild our life. The money I earned at my prison job was minimal—it would take months to save up enough to purchase shoes on commissary. Everything on commissary sold for retail prices even though our wages were less than a dollar an hour. It seemed hopeless.

But even as a child, I knew God could surprise me with a gentle reminder of His presence. This time in my life was no exception. In prison, we had four 'counts' every day—times when we lined up and stood silent in the doorway while the guards counted heads. During this particular count, I opened the door of my cell and incredibly, there they were: purple tennis shoes! Not just any tennis shoes, but my favorite color of tennis shoes—purple! Right outside my door, under the stairway!

A truly wonderful thing you never hear about women in prison—there is a generosity of Spirit that is difficult to comprehend. Women who have almost nothing always seem to find something to share. If a woman received two blankets and only needed one, she would put her extra blanket under the stairway, which was a type of 'store' where you took only what you needed and gave what extra you possessed. You might even find a book, or an extra pillow, a shirt, a pair of pants. But this was the first and only time I had ever found shoes. And they fit perfectly.

It was like a gift—not only from one of my sisters at FCI Pleasanton, but also from a God who never abandons, never forgets. My heart swelled once again with joy for the One Who heard my unspoken need. I thought of my favorite verse, "And God is able to make all grace abound toward you, so that you, always having all sufficiency in all things, may have an abundance for every good work."[21]

That was my God—abounding toward me with a grace that would carry me through. And in this case, He was wearing purple tennis shoes.

---

[21] 2 Corinthians 9:8

THE BUTTERFLY COMETH

Day 167:   TASTING LIFE

Life is like a slot machine. The coins you put into it are work and ideas. And, unlike a Las Vegas slot machine, you can influence the chances of winning with your will. Bessie Copage

Our taste buds are very conducive assets. They enable us to detect the flavorless, the flat, or the stale and evoke the option to produce a scrumptious, palatable feast.

Take, for instance, hamburgers—American's beloved favorite food. Centuries ago, the Russians adopted the custom of shredding raw beef for an entrée. They livened it up with onion juice and salt and pepper. German sailors found the dish equally appetizing and brought the recipe home with them to Hamburg. The locals refused to eat the uncooked meat believing only savages devoured raw animal products so they broiled it. The dish made its way to the United States where Americans added a bun. What began as a K-ration evolved into a mouth-watering way of life.

There are days when we wake up and feel like a dull piece of ground beef. That doesn't mean that the entire day will be blue. With a few dashes of allspice, we can take command of our world and become a glorified ground top round.

Whether we enjoy ours with Swiss, Worcestershire, or crowned in Heinz 57, we will relish in the sauce of a red Bordeaux broil. This completeness may be just the nudge love's taste buds need to meld the sweet sensation of sacred wholeness with the tart recruits of lethargic lack of interest.

This day, meld.

Day 168:   IT'S MORE THAN SKIN DEEP

The empty bag cannot stand up. Haitian proverb

It was August 28, 2005, and Hurricane Katrina was brewing in the Gulf of Mexico. As she stormed New Orleans and Biloxi, thousands of people lost their homes and hundreds lost their lives. With those losses, so too, died a part of the bonhomie of the south.

DIANA LOUISE WEBB

Many ask, "If there is a God, why did He let such life, beauty and enchantment pass away?"

In the short-term, the question is interesting. *How could a God who loves us so much allow devastation to dominate?* When we look around at the ruins, to answer this question, we have to see under the crust just like we have to see under our own skin to interpret the intricate workings which enable our bodies to function as Christ's innovation. The obvious does not always suggest quenching explanations. It is what lies beneath an outward manifestation that cradles the answers.

Think about the Indian art of constructing ornate rugs. On the back of a tapestry in progress, strings hang and flutter in total disarray. Loose ends with frayed edges, it is a muddled mess. But when we turn over the decorative craft, an astonishing picture comes to life.

On that same stratum, God will not let anything take place which will not result in something awesome and beautiful even though the overlay charades a crisis zone.

Katrina raged ashore. She wiped out businesses, hospitals, homes, restaurants and historical monuments. In one section of her course, 200-year-old oak trees that once stoutly resided as symbols of southern charm, uprooted. In their midst stood a statue of our Lord Jesus assembled on a pedestal. Although not anchored to its base, the sculpture neither toppled nor washed out to the sea during the ferocious storm. It remained standing—a message to the faithful that God's love prevails; a message that under the wreckage, we are a nation that won't give up on the "mother lode." Our beauty is more than skin-deep.

Be it nature's shrink-wrap, husk, bark, rind or coat of a tropical cyclone, internal beauty outdistances the outer shell and creates new external beauty pleasing to God. Augustin Guillerand captured this concept in acquainting us with his perception that, "Every creature gifted with reason has received light to see in all created things both their own individual beauty and that of the Supreme Being, from whom they received their being, and who sustains them in it. With the light given us we can see God in all things and come into harmony."

Don't frown upon life's brusque mantle. The "mother lode" waits. Simply love a little stronger and dig a little deeper.

THE BUTTERFLY COMETH

<u>Day 169</u>:   SEEING BEYOND THE CORNEA

Love has given humans very real gifts. The chief one is the divine indwelling, God's own presence within us, sustaining us by this creative action and embracing us. Thomas Keating

A popular allegory speaks of an elderly man who hobbled to a neighboring well every morning to fill his daily water needs. The heavy crossbar he lugged around his neck courted two buckets, one on each side. The left one bore a small fissure from which half the water trickled out as he ambled back home.

One day on the morning water run, the cracked bucket spoke, "Kind sir, you are so hardworking. I regret I can only give you fifty percent."

The man replied, "My dear little helper, you give me far more than you realize. Look around. See that glorious row of flowers gracing the road in front of my house?"

Sure enough, there were candytufts and magnolias, zinnias and geraniums, and daffodils and cornflowers. White butterflies polkaed amid the photographic panorama. Chubby bumblebees outfitted in black and yellow tuxedos hummed softly as they sashayed across the colorful, floral ballroom, bathing in the liquid light of the botanical providence.

The man resumed, "You water these beauties everyday as we walk which makes such splendor possible. Without the water you provide, there would be no flowers."

This story is an unforgettable example of how God takes what is broken down and kaput and converts it into timeless finery. We may not see how co-operation with Heavenly wisdom works for the greater good unless we call upon our inner eye: the light given us, so we can see God in all things.

In the book, <u>Waiting For God</u>, writer Simone Weil cites that "all love of universal beauty proceeds from God dwelling in our souls and goes out to God present in the universe." It is love that revives us to a reality which matters—an all-transcendent meaning of life. To think otherwise is blindness indicative that we need more than just our windows washed.

DIANA LOUISE WEBB

One of the advantages of life is the miracle of being human—that our eyes can see a variety of approximately 8,000,000 colors. Yet, we continue to live a bland, beaten existence. So what will set us ablaze? What will enable us to see from the outside in? The answer may be found in listening from the inside out.

Macrina Wiederkehr's <u>Seasons Of Your Heart</u> emphasizes how we are challenged to live by one simple commitment: "If you should ever hear God speaking to you from a burning bush, and it happens more often than most of us realize, take off your shoes for the ground on which you stand is holy."

See with holy eyes.
Listen with a holy heart.
Live by holy principles.

You'll see it. Just look ...

<u>Day 170</u>:   WHAT'S YOUR CONNECTION?

Those who love deeply never grow old; they may die of old age, but they die young. Dramatist Arthur Wing Pinero

As we behold the miracle of the human body, we cannot help but notice how one limb interacts with another to form a perfect workable part—a useful member of a whole which provides a service. As we nourish each delicate structure, we cherish it as an irreplaceable fresco.

Nothing rang more true than when I broke my ankle during a softball game fifteen years ago. I slid into home base for an out-of-this-world grand slam. Ill-timed (and ill-fated), more than home plate took a beating.

Diagnosed with a hairline fracture, I spent six weeks laid up as a couch potato. Without the use of my ankle, I couldn't walk as nothing connected my leg to my foot.

This is similar to each area of our lives working its best when all components swing in concurrence with one another. The nucleus of harmony expressed is love and love makes all things possible. An interdependency and mutual respect for all components of our lifestyle, when employed daily, assure a long, balanced, worthy and pleasing life on earth.

Everything has a place in moderation. Too much or too little is comparable to a broken ankle: a connection isn't made. Therefore, pieces are missing which render optimal performance impossible. Pieces of our lives suffer.

What pieces are missing from your life? What are you going to do about it?

<u>Day 171</u>:   YOU DON'T HAVE TO BE AN ATHLETE TO FLEX

Dream lofty dreams, and as you dream, so shall you become. Your vision is the promise of what you shall one day be. James Allen

As the last day of this book journey ends, we come to the realization that putting color back into our lives is really opening up to what has been there all along: hidden blessings obscured by brooms shades. Behind the veneers are all of our goals, desires, talents and aspirations—grand masterpieces waiting to be unleashed.

Love is our backing force. It is with us always. Love offers Light, Opportunity, Victory and Eternity. Fear-free and faith-filled, we are refreshed to the notion of 'anticipate and accelerate.' By maintaining the ultimate standard of goodness for which we were created, we are free to live the fairytale God envisioned for us. We don't always have to have the new and improved. A wrinkle in our skin does not cause a wrinkle in our soul or a wrinkle in time. Most of what is important has weathered the centuries and the crux still holds true today: we are either cultivating joy or we are not.

The soul was made for an end, a gracious good. Serving as a quiet holy reminder to set our sights high, the soul cannot thrive without a wellspring to supply its lifeblood. The French scientist, Blaise Pascal, wrote about this wellspring affirming, "There was once in man a true happiness, of which there now remains to him only an empty trace which he vainly tries to fill out of his environment. Yet all these efforts are inadequate, because the infinite abyss can only be filled by an infinite and immutable object, that is, by God Himself."

DIANA LOUISE WEBB

Therefore, Make your Mark! A recurrent phrase that is not just for the outgoing and overachievers, "Make your Mark!" connotes taking a stride victoriously upward. The success train is available to all. It stops to pick up everyone who chooses to jump aboard. Any limits imposed are self-imposed by the seven deadlies: (1) Boasting and spending too much money; (2) Neglecting family, friends and self; (3) Indolence on the job; (4) Infidelity; (5) Overindulging; (6) Fearing the unknown; and, (7) Malice.

We hatch our present, which becomes our tomorrow. Author C. S. Lewis shares the reality of what is looming over life. He suggests, "The future is something which everyone reaches at the rate of sixty minutes an hour, whatever they do, whoever they are." It is our decision to labor in the multihued hours using the amazing imagination God gave us or to idly wash out into an achromatic stupor.

Created to live in principled excellence, we owe it to ourselves to fly right through the panel of impossibilities. The imperishable cameo of our determination provides us with the strength. That durability is not our innate potency as natural strength commands no faith. No, it is the power to believe without seeing. It is knowing "this ain't it" and that we don't just die and rot in the ground. It is realizing we have a purpose—an important mission; that the world was created for a reason. It is recognizing that sometime after our "final appointment," we will come to know why all that happened to us *happened to us* and why material riches are obsolete and why all the "stuff" we worried about and collected while here really was not as vital as we thought it was.

Once we pick up the quest to live, as God wants us to live, we enjoy a rebirth—the coming of our spiritual butterfly: total and sweet. Explanations will be provided much later. We were created to live in the present. God wants every day to count. Of course, events will happen all the time, which simply are not right. Sometimes, "it is what it is." Injustice, travail and bloodshed may still masquerade as fairness, equity and honor, but grace will prevail if we don't slip off the serving platter.

Flex! Make your Mark!

Love unconditionally. Be grateful. Give back. Quash rumors. Accept differences. Celebrate with a glad heart. Direct your thoughts

THE BUTTERFLY COMETH

to peaceful paths. Blot out the darkness. Rise up—steadfast and sure. Be merciful. Forgive. Tenderly set free your colorful butterfly. Become a living presence to the world—total and sweet.

Total and sweet!

SOURCES

Bibles

Good News Bible. New York: American Bible Society, 1978.

Holy Bible. Tennessee: Omega Publishing House, 1969.

The New American Bible. New York: Catholic Book Publishing Co., 1970.

Books

Bellugi, Ursula and Klima Edward. The Signs of Language. Massachusetts: Harvard University Press, 1979.

Brinegar, Jerry. Breaking Free from Domestic Violence. Minnesota: CompCare Publishers, 1992.

Challoner, Jack. The Visual Dictionary of Physics. New York, NY: DK Publishing, 1995.

Daly, Kathleen. Greek and Roman Mythology A-Z. New York: Facts on File, 1992.

Ellis, Albert and Velten, Emmett. <u>When AA Doesn't Work for You: A Rational Guide for Quitting Alcohol</u>. New York, NY: Barricade Books, 1962.

Francis, Valerie. <u>Illustrated Guide to Dreams</u>. Connecticut: Brompton Books Corp., 1995.

Hurley, Joanne. <u>Mother Teresa 1910-1997: A Pictorial Biography</u>. Pennsylvania: Courage Books, 1997.

Johnson, Barbara. <u>I'm So Glad You Told Me What I Didn't Wanna Hear</u>. Texas: Word Publishing, 1996.

Kelly, Kathy. <u>Other Lands Have Dreams: From Baghdad to Pekin Prison</u>. A K Press, 2005. By permission.

Kranz, Rachel. <u>The Biographical Dictionary of Black Americans</u>. New York, NY: Facts on File, 1992.

Ralston, Aron. <u>Between a Rock and a Hard Place</u>. Aron Ralston, 2004. By permission.

<u>Readers Digest Book of Facts</u>. New York: Reader's Digest Association, Inc., 1985.

<u>The Dictionary of Music</u>. New Lanark, Scotland: Geddes & Grosset Ltd., 1995.

Walker, Richard. <u>The Visual Dictionary of Human Anatomy</u>. New York, NY: DK Publishing, 1996.

Wexler, Sanford. <u>The Civil Rights Movement</u>. New York: Facts on File, 1993.

Whitaker, Carl. <u>From Psyche to System: The Evolving Therapy of Carl Whitaker</u>. New York, NY: Guilford Press, 1982.

THE BUTTERFLY COMETH

Internet Resources

Center for Auto Safety. <u>Ford Pinto Fuel-Fed Fires</u>.
http://www.autosafety.org/article.php?did=522&scid=96

Davis, Leonard. <u>Private Spaceship Encounters Glitches in Record-Setting Flight</u>.
http://www.space.com/missionlaunches/SS1_press_040621.html
(June 21st, 2004)

Short Stories

Rios, Richie. <u>Time</u>. Richie Rios, 2008. By permission.

Video

Barkan, Jonathan and Rosen, Ellsworth (Co-Producers). <u>Bearing Witness: American Soldiers and the Holocaust</u>. [film] Arlington, MA: Communications for Learning, 2001.

Beugen-Bishop, Suzy (Producer). <u>The Miracle Worker</u>. [film] Burbank, CA: Buena Vista Home Entertainment, 2000.

DonVito, Paul (Exe. Producer). <u>World Trade Center: Anatomy of the Collapse</u>. [film] Santa Monica, CA: Artisan Entertainment, Inc., 2002.

Schnall, Peter (Exe. Producer). <u>New York Firefighters: The Brotherhood of 9/11</u>. [film] Santa Monica, CA: Artisan Entertainment, Inc., 2002.

Searchinger, Gene (Producer/Director). <u>In A Brilliant Light: Van Gogh In Arles</u>. [film] New York, NY: The Office of Film and Television of the Metropolitan Museum of Art, 1984.

www.ingramcontent.com/pod-product-compliance
Lightning Source LLC
LaVergne TN
LVHW022241090126
829240LV00001B/1